HOW
The Secret
CHANGED
MY LIFE

Also by Rhonda Byrne

The Secret

The Secret Gratitude Book

The Secret Daily Teachings

The Power

The Magic

Hero

Also from The Secret

The Secret to Teen Power
by Paul Harrington

The Power of Henry's Imagination
by Skye Byrne and Nic George

HOW
The Secret
CHANGED
MY LIFE

Real People. Real Stories.

SIMON &
SCHUSTER

London · New York · Sydney · Toronto · New Delhi

A CBS COMPANY

First published in Great Britain by Simon & Schuster UK Ltd, 2016
A CBS COMPANY

10 9 8 7 6 5 4 3 2 1

Simon & Schuster UK Ltd
1st Floor
222 Gray's Inn Road
London WC1X 8HB

www.simonandschuster.co.uk
www.simonandschuster.com.au
www.simonandschuster.co.in

Simon & Schuster Australia, Sydney
Simon & Schuster India, New Delhi

**The information contained in this book is intended to be educational and not for diagnosis,
prescription or treatment of any health disorders or as a substitute for financial planning.
This information should not replace consultation with a competent healthcare or financial
professional. The content of this book is intended to be used as an adjunct to a rational and
responsible programme prescribed by a healthcare practitioner or financial professional.
The author and publisher are in no way liable for any misuse of the material.**

A CIP catalogue record for this book is available from the British Library

Hardback ISBN: 978-1-4711-5819-3
eBook ISBN: 978-1-4711-5820-9

Jacket design by Nic George for Making Good LLC and
Albert Tang, art director for Atria Books
Book design concept by Nic George for Making Good LLC
Interior design by Suet Y. Chong

Printed and bound in Italy by L.E.G.O. SpA

Simon & Schuster UK Ltd are committed to sourcing paper that is made from wood grown in
sustainable forests and support the Forest Stewardship Council®, the leading international forest
certification organisation. Our books displaying the FSC® logo are printed on FSC certified paper.

*Dedicated to
the one and only
you*

Contents

Introduction

Since *The Secret* was released to the world, tens of thousands of people have written to us to share the story of how they used The Secret principles to attract what they wanted: health, wealth, the perfect partner, the perfect career, a restored marriage or relationship, to bring back something that was lost, even to replace depression with happiness. By following the methods in *The Secret*, these people – from every culture and country across the planet – have transformed their life from what it was to something extraordinary. They did what the average person would have said is impossible. But these people knew that *nothing* is impossible.

Featured in this book are some of the most miraculous,

uplifting, and inspiring real-life Secret Stories chosen from those we've received in the last ten years, and together they will take you on an unforgettable journey that will break the limits of your mind. These stories clearly demonstrate that no matter who you are, no matter where you are, you can use The Secret to create whatever it is you want.

Along with the Secret Stories, my words will guide you throughout the pages of this book with The Secret's wisdom. If you're new to The Secret, this will give you a comprehensive understanding of how to use its principles. If you're already familiar with The Secret, it will act as a reminder of the simple things you can do to have a good life filled with everything you want.

Over the years I have been able to manifest all the desires on my seemingly never-ending list, but without a doubt, hearing from people about the miraculous ways they have changed their own lives has been the greatest gift The Secret has given me personally. Material objects and material things are great fun, and you should have whatever it is that you want, but being able to do something to help another human being have a better life brings with it a happiness that can never leave you. And ultimately, happiness is all that we ever want.

I want you to know how easily you can change your life, and it's not by running around trying to force it into the shape you want. You change your life in the only way you can ever change it: change your mind, and then your life will change.

Rhonda Byrne

There are two kinds of people:
Those who say,
"I will believe it when I see it."
And those who say,
"To see it, I know I must believe it."

– The Secret Daily Teachings

How I Asked, Believed, and Received: The Creative Process

The great secret of life is the law of attraction, which says that like attracts like. What this means for you is that you are attracting into your life the experiences and circumstances that are *like* the thoughts and images you're holding in your mind. Whatever you constantly think about, you will attract into your life.

If you think about what you want, and continue to think about it, you will bring it into your life. Through this most powerful law, your thoughts become the things in your life. Your current thoughts are creating your future life, and so by changing your thoughts now, you can change your life.

Once you understand The Secret, you can then use the Creative Process to attract whatever you want and live the life of your dreams. The Creative Process is made up of three simple steps: Ask, Believe, Receive.

First Ask

The law of attraction responds to any consistent thought you hold in your mind. Even if you ask for something extremely specific, you needn't have any doubt that you'll receive exactly what you asked for.

SINGING WITH STEVIE WONDER

Hi all, my name is John Pereira, and this is how *The Secret* worked for me. First of all, at the time I wasn't doing too well, I was depressed and angry, mainly with a business partner my sister and I had. My sister had been pestering me to watch *The Secret,* and one day she made us all stop what we were doing and watch the movie. From that day on, I decided to give it a go and just practice it.

Two days later, I was at the gym reading the paper and noticed a concert date for Stevie Wonder on the 22nd of October, which is also my birthday. I said to my sister, "This is it. I'm not going to just meet him; I'm going to sing with him!"

I told everyone that I had met George Benson, I had partied with Jamiroquai, and now I was going to sing with the head honcho himself, Stevie. Everyone thought I was crazy. The next day when I was visiting my brother, I got up to make him coffee and asked him to pause the program we were watching on television. When I came back into the room, the screen was paused on WIN THE CHANCE TO SING LIVE ONSTAGE WITH STEVIE WONDER. I couldn't believe it!

I went straight home to enter. You had to write in twenty words why you wanted to sing with Stevie, and words just flew out of my brain. After I submitted it, I asked my girlfriend if I should submit again. Just at that moment the computer crashed and never worked again. "Don't worry," I said to her, "this is mine, I don't need to enter it again!"

A week or so had passed, and I was out having drinks with some friends. I looked over at one of my mates and said, "Do you know I'm going to sing with Stevie Wonder?" Again, another person looking at me as if I'm crazy.

The very next day I went home after work and said to my sister, "What am I going to do when I sing with him?" She said, "Just remember to take your time, because it will be over before you know it, so savor the moment." I was about to have an afternoon nap when my phone started ringing. I answered it, and the guy says, "Is this John Pereira? And did you enter a competition?" I replied, "Yes." He said, "Well, congratulations, you're the national winner!" I screamed and started throwing my girlfriend in the air. I called my parents and screamed. I called my sister and started screaming. I called my brother and started screaming. And the friend I'd told the night before just replied, "Yeah, yeah" when I told him. He could not believe it.

So, if anyone doesn't believe, BELIEVE! I'm living proof, and if you would like to watch it, here is the YouTube clip: http://www.youtube.com/watch?v=IMftLNs_G6M.

~ *John P.*, Sydney, Australia

Here's another amazing example of someone attracting a very specific desire using The Secret.

IT'S A MIRACLE

I found out about *The Secret* from *The Oprah Winfrey Show*. I truly believed every single word written in the book and spoken on the video. Then I received an email from *The Secret* giving me a link to download a check from the Bank of the Universe. So I downloaded the check and wrote an amount of one hundred thousand ringgit [Malaysian currency equaling about $25,000 U.S.] on it just for fun, and I pinned it to the small vision board near my dressing table.

Then I took a one-ringgit bill and added zeros with a marker. I wanted to write 100,000.00, but the space was so small that I managed to add just five zeros. It ended up looking like 1,000.00, but I didn't want to throw it away, so I just put it up there on my vision board with the check.

I looked at it every day and told myself that I believed it would happen. I didn't really know whether my visualization exercise was correct, but I just did it every once in a while. And to be frank, as time went by, I kind of forgot about it.

Then, in early October, when I was paying my credit card bill at the service counter, I saw a pamphlet about a contest called "RM100,000.00 Dream Catcher SMS contest" that the credit card company was running. It started on July 5 and ended on October 15, but this was the first I'd heard about it. Then I thought, *Well, I still have two weeks to send my entry; better late than never.* So I did.

Then, at the end of the month, I received a call from the credit card company telling me that I had won second prize for the month of October. For that, I would get a cash prize of RM1,000.00. I was thrilled, because I've never really had much luck in big contests. I told my husband, and we were jumping with joy.

Two months after that, I received another call from the company, saying that I had been selected as one of eleven finalists to compete for the grand prize of RM100,000.00 and that the winner would be decided the following week.

That night I was sitting at my dressing table when I noticed my vision board. There was the RM100,000.00 check I had written three months before. My heart was beating fast as I noticed the one-ringgit bill that looked like RM1,000 rather than RM100,000.00.

I took the note and the check into the living room to show my husband. I said, "Sweetheart, I think I know why I won second prize for RM1,000. It's the RM1 bill! Even though I ordered it by accident, God still delivered it to me! It's The Secret in action!"

Then I was crying tears of happiness. The little voice inside of me kept saying I'd be the winner of the grand prize, that God (the Universe) had arranged the event, people, and circumstances to deliver my RM100,000.00 check to me.

Then I read the chapter on The Secret to Money and watched the video again. Every time I had a doubt that the prize was mine, I quickly replaced it with the image of me on the stage, smiling and holding the big mock check for RM100,000.00.

Before we left the house on the morning of the grand finale, my husband said to me, "Take the RM100,000.00 check that you wrote; you're going to claim the real one today." So I did.

Before entering the room, I took a last look at that check, visualized winning, and tried to cast off doubt. Then I noticed the remittance advice on top of the check: FEEL GOOD. I quickly grabbed my husband's iPhone and opened the photo albums of my beautiful two-year-old daughter. Seeing her sweet smile made me feel so happy inside that I knew I was on the right track. Throughout the whole event, I just thought about my daughter's smile and visualized winning.

And YES I DID!

I won the grand prize of RM100,000.00. When they announced my name, I felt as if I were having a déjà vu experience, because I'd had the same pictures rolling in my mind so many times before.

After delivering the mock check, the judge said to me, "When you walked into this room with the other ten finalists, you looked the happiest of all. Maybe that's because you knew that you were going to win."

So it really is a miracle. I wrote a bill for RM1,000.00 by accident and a check for RM100,000.00 on August 18, and on December 12, they both came true.

When I told my friends and family what had happened, those with doubts became believers.

~ *Enny*, Kuala Lumpur, Malaysia

It may feel as if what you want is almost impossible to receive. But for the law of attraction, nothing is impossible and everything is possible, even if you're asking for a miracle, as was the case with the story of Popeye, the runaway pug.

POPEYE

My twenty-one-year-old daughter and her dog, Popeye, a four-year-old male pug, had been living with us for four months, and I was Popeye's caretaker during that time. When my daughter moved out, she took my beloved Popeye with her, and we didn't hear from her for about two months. When I asked about Popeye, she told me that he had escaped from the yard at the house where she was staying and she could not find him.

I made up a flyer, took it to the copy shop, and had a hundred copies made. I put up posters all around the area where Popeye went missing. When I asked how long he'd been gone, my daughter said a month. I was shocked that she had not told us sooner. Statistics will tell you that if you don't find an animal within the first three weeks, you most likely will not find him at all.

I received several phone calls about a pug in the area, and I always ran to wherever the caller said they had seen him. Then one day a caller said they had a male pug, so I rushed to the address only to find that it was not my baby. As time went by, I put up more and more flyers but got fewer and fewer phone calls. I put an ad in the paper and searched the neighborhood, spoke with people, and handed out more flyers.

Until then I did not know about *The Secret*. It came into my life when I took my son to Mississippi State University for a college visit and went to the bookstore on campus. The first time we went in, I purchased several items but not *The Secret*. I didn't even see the book. But later that day my son wanted something else, so we went back to the store, and as we were getting in line to check out, I saw *The Secret*. I had no idea what it was, but the cover struck me, so I purchased it. After the weekend was over, I took the book home and began reading it. Then I realized why Popeye was not home yet. When he left, I put his bed in the garage. It had been in my closet, but it hurt me to look at it. I put the bed back in the closet, and I went to the vet and got his food. I still put up posters, but I also said thanks daily for Popeye being home. I so believed he was home that I would cry because I was so thankful.

For a couple of weeks, there were no calls of any kind, yet I never lost faith. Then one day I got a call from someone saying they had seen a pug in the area. At the time they saw him, Popeye had been lost only a couple of weeks, but they just wanted me to know there was still hope. I thought that was wonderful of them. Then a few hours later I received another call, and this man told me that Popeye was in Texas with his niece. He said that she had been visiting at the time Popeye went missing and had found him by the school, which was very close to where he escaped. She had walked around the neighborhood asking if anyone knew him but found no one. So when it came time for her to go home, she took him with her. Her uncle had been traveling for several months, so when he came home and saw my flyers around town, he called his niece and told her that Popeye's family was hunting for him. He gave me her number, and I called and asked if the dog she had did Popeye's trick, and sure enough, he did.

Now, you may be wondering how I would get Popeye back when he was in Texas and I was in Mississippi. Well, the rest of the story is that she lived fifteen minutes from my father, who picked up Popeye and is bringing him home to me when he comes for my son's graduation!

~ *Marta*, Mississippi, USA

Marta knew she had to get herself to the place of believing Popeye was home, which is no easy feat when a dearly loved pet is lost. She chose to take specific actions that were very powerful – such as bringing his bed back into her closet and buying his food – because those actions said that Popeye had returned home. Marta's belief became so strong that it even caused her to weep with gratitude that Popeye had returned. That kind of belief is the second vital step in the Creative Process.

The Second Step: Believe

Ask, believe, receive – just three simple steps to create what you want. However, very often the second step, believe, can be the most difficult, yet it is the greatest step you will ever take. Believing contains no doubt. Believing does not waver. Believing is absolute faith. Believing remains steadfast despite what is happening in the outside world.

When you master believing, you have mastered your life.

– The Secret Daily Teachings

I BELIEVE!

About six months ago, my boyfriend and I spontaneously decided to move to another city where he had lived before. He went ahead and moved in with his friend so that it would be easier for him to look for a job. It was hard for me, of course, because I missed him so, but I had already given notice at my job and planned to follow him a month later.

As time went by, however, nothing seemed to be working out. My boyfriend did not get the job he wanted, so he had been out of work for nearly a month. I had not found a new job either, and on top of that, I couldn't find anyone to take over my apartment. If I didn't find someone who could move in the day I was moving out, I would have to pay another three months' rent, which we could not afford. My boyfriend and I were miles apart. I was lonely and almost desperate. Time and money seemed to be running out on us.

One weekend when I was visiting him, we found an apartment. But then we learned that the family who still lived there wouldn't be able to move out until a few days after we were scheduled to move in. We had already scheduled the movers and couldn't change the date. It all seemed to be a mess.

When I was really desperate and in tears one night about a week before the final move, I read *The Secret*. I chose two stones to be my gratitude stones, and while holding the stones in one hand, with the other I wrote down everything I was thankful for in my life and everything I wanted, especially for moving into my new life. I wished for a job, and for a vacation too. I wanted to find a job immediately, but I also wanted to have time to get to know the city and settle into our new apartment. I wished for a job for my boyfriend, and I wished that we could move into our apartment on the weekend we had planned and not one day later! I printed out two pictures of the house we were supposed to be moving into and wrote in big red numbers the date I wanted to move in. I carried one picture with me and put the other beside my bed. Also, I wished for a nice girl to move into my apartment on the day I would be leaving.

I started carrying the stones in my jeans pocket so that every time I touched them, I thought about the list of things I had written that night.

And guess what happened! A girl called me about five days before I was going to leave, saying that she wanted to move into my apartment. And she even bought my washing machine, which I couldn't take with me and wanted to sell. My boyfriend and I moved into our new apartment on the weekend we had planned, and we had two weeks to feel at home in our beautiful new city before we both signed contracts for new jobs on the same day!

I am so grateful for getting to know *The Secret* and myself better. It does work; all you need to do is believe, especially in yourself. It continues to help me every day. Thank you, Rhonda, for sharing *The Secret* with us. I'll keep on sharing it too.

~ *Nia*, Germany

You must know that what you want is yours the moment you ask. You must have complete and utter faith. You must act, speak, and think as though you have it *now*. That is what it means to believe.

Nia used the pictures of her new house with the move-in date written on them to reinforce her belief that she *already had it*. Whenever you get yourself to this place of believing, the Universe must move all people, circumstances, and events for you to receive! How it will happen, *how* the Universe will bring it to you, is not your concern or job. Allow the Universe to do it for you. When you try to work out *how* it will happen, you are emitting a frequency that contains a lack of faith – that you don't believe you have it already. You think *you* have to do it, and you do not believe the Universe will do it *for* you.

A GREEN CARD MIRACLE

In January 2011, I bought *The Secret* at a tiny bookstore at the airport while I was waiting to board my flight back to the USA from my hometown in Kerala, India. Reading it on the plane back to L.A. changed my life forever. I had struggled with negativity my entire life, but the teachings of *The Secret* helped me to change my outlook and take control of my future.

But I still fell off the wagon many times. I often overlooked the blessings of my new job, beautiful new home, and great new relationship, and focused on the things I did not have – in particular, a permanent green card that would allow me to continue living in the States.

I had a temporary green card based on my short-lived marriage, but to get a permanent one I would have to prove that the marriage was real and still valid. The marriage had been real enough – I had the emotional scars to prove it – but my husband and I had separated barely a year after our wedding and were on our way to finalizing the divorce.

I had to hire an immigration lawyer, which was expensive, and all I did was gripe about how much all this was costing and the fact that I was going to be deported. As a result, the law of attraction ensured that my problems continued.

Things were going from bad to worse when I decided to visit The Secret site and read some of the testimonials to change the funk I was in. I was inspired by the many people who had written about their personal miracles and decided to get back on the wagon right away. I printed two color copies of my current green card and changed the expiration date from 2011 to 2021. I pinned a copy to my corkboard at work where I could see it and put the other one in my wallet.

And then I did something that ensured the success of my wish: I forgot all about it! I did not spend another minute thinking about the process, what the lawyers were up to, whether I had given enough supporting documents – not a single negative thought. I also did not try to "help" the process along, as I normally would have done. I did not imagine my interview with the immigration officer going well; I did not spend any thought on my lawyer providing brilliant arguments in my favor. I quite simply let it go. Whenever someone asked me how it was going, I shrugged and said my application was being processed. I refused to follow up with my lawyer's office or fret over the date by which I should have heard back about an appointment with the immigration officer.

With my understanding of how the visa process works, logically, I would have at best envisioned a brief interview, a successful meeting with an immigration officer who was inclined to like me, and so on. But the law of attraction gave me more than I could ever have imagined! On the first day of June, two months before my current card expired, I received my new green card in the mail. No interview, no immigration officer, no meeting, no follow-up, just the card with the expiration date 2022 printed on it: one year MORE than I had written on my inspiration copy!

What I learned from this experience is that often the answer is not to strive constantly to think only positive thoughts about something we want; it's the ability to ask, believe, and then let go. Trusting that the Universe has received my wish, being confident that I have articulated it clearly, and believing that my wish will be granted are the three steps I have mastered. I am still working on resisting the urge to keep trying to fine-tune my request or help it along by adding more positive vibes.

~ *Ambika N.,* Los Angeles, California, USA

As Ambika came to realize, when you're feeling good, it's much easier to believe you'll receive your desire than if you're not feeling good. That's because believing is a positive emotion, and it's on the same frequency as feeling good. So don't try to practice believing if you're feeling down in the dumps. Get yourself feeling good, then do the visualizing and practices that will help you believe.

If you are complaining about things in your life, you are on the complaining frequency, and you are not in a position to attract what you want.

Get on to the frequency of good with your thoughts and words. Firstly you will feel good, and secondly you will be on the frequency of receiving more good.

– The Secret Daily Teachings

ASK ONCE AND LET IT GO

My husband and I had decided to purchase a new home and leave our current home empty until it sold. It was a very big gamble given the crash of the real estate market, but we were feeling optimistic. However, after more than twenty open houses in seven months with no offers, I was getting very discouraged and really stressed about having to carry two mortgages.

I first learned about *The Secret* while watching *The Oprah Winfrey Show.* Shortly after that, I encouraged my husband to watch the movie with me on our computer. That was on a Friday. On Sunday I had to go over to the empty house and clean out the garage, and at that point I decided to use what I had learned by watching *The Secret*. I asked once for the sale of the house, I visualized a sale-pending sign, I felt grateful, and I let it go.

As I was closing the garage and about to return to my car, I saw a gentleman picking up a flyer from the for-sale sign on my lawn. The next day my Realtor called to let us know that we had three offers on the house. We closed escrow 45 days later.

~ *Tricia,* Brentwood, California, USA

Ask, Believe, and You Will *Receive*

LIFELONG DREAMS OF TRAVEL

For as long as I can remember, I have wanted to travel. In my opinion, there is no greater blessing than to see the world and experience everything the earth has to offer. I remember journaling about it when I was in high school, basically declaring that I was going to travel someday. I realize now that back then I was using The Secret but just didn't know it. My first goal, however, was to finish college.

Living during the recession in the USA was very spirit-crushing and at times very frustrating. I never would have guessed that I would be graduating college during the biggest economic crisis since the Great Depression! I had *no* money, I had student loans, and I couldn't find a job in my little college town to save my life. Either nobody was hiring or my school schedule didn't fit with the job. I was starting to feel really discouraged.

I had read *The Secret* and applied it to some things, but I don't think I *really and truly* believed in it with all my heart. So I decided to read it again, and this time it really hit home.

I had three and a half months before graduation to manifest traveling while the world around me screamed, "You will never be able to travel!" Even my parents, who are amazing and supportive people, told me, "Get those dreams of travel out of your head . . . it's not going to happen for a long time. You have no money, and we aren't paying for it!" At times it was hard not to just give in and say, "Oh, they're right." Instead I shook my head and decided to stop talking to them about it, because they were being so negative. Meanwhile I kept telling myself every single day, "I am going to travel. I don't know how or when, but it *will* happen."

I made a vision board with pictures of places I wanted to go. I journaled every single night, listing everything in my life I was grateful for – things I loved about people, things I loved about myself, etc. I would write about how grateful I was to get the opportunity to see the world, and what great things it would do for my soul. After weeks and weeks of journaling, it really helped me to feel as if I had already received it. I honestly believed with a full heart that it would happen for me.

Then, about a month and a half into practicing this, I got an email from an old friend offering me a position in Italy – a cultural exchange to live with a family! The family then contacted me and offered to *pay* me to live there. I couldn't believe it. This opportunity literally *fell* into my lap.

After that I thought, *Okay, so once I am there, I'll have money. Now I just need to figure out how to get there!* I kept telling myself I was going *for sure;* I just needed money for my plane ticket.

A few weeks later, I graduated college, and lo and behold, people started sending me graduation money. All the money added up to the exact amount I needed for my ticket.

After that, I realized that I couldn't go all the way to Italy and see *only* Italy. I wanted to see a lot more of Europe. So

I decided that I would spend my last month backpacking around. My friends and family were concerned, asking, "How will you save that much money? Are you going to go alone? Who's going to go with you?" But I kept insisting, "I will figure it out when the time comes. I will have someone to travel with, and I will save enough money. I just know it!"

So I booked my return ticket based on staying that extra month, and *the very next day* my best friend, who was living in another state, called me to catch up. We hadn't talked in a long time. When I told her about my plans to travel in Europe, she immediately said, "I'm going with you. I am booking my ticket now . . . See you in Rome!"

My *entire* trip was manifested through using The Secret. It's a beautiful feeling to know that something so wonderful can happen to you just by changing your own thoughts! My trip was a life-changing experience, I had more than enough money to do it, and by the end, I even had money left over!

It really is true: Ask, Believe, Receive. It really does work.

Thank you, thank you, thank you! Good blessings to all.

~ *Ashley S.,* Seattle, Washington, USA

Ask once, believe you have received, and all you have to do to receive is feel good. When you are feeling good, you are on the frequency of receiving. You are on the frequency of all good things coming to you, and you will receive what you have asked for.

A fast way to get yourself on that frequency is to say, "I am receiving now. I am receiving all the good in my life now. I am receiving [fill in the blank] now." And *feel* it. *Feel* it as though you have received.

That's what Ashley did with her journaling, and acting *as if* she had received made her both a believer and a receiver!

Ask for Something Small

Most people can manifest the small things quickly. This is because they do not have any resistance around the small things, and because they don't think thoughts that contradict them. When it comes to the bigger things, however, people often emit thoughts of doubt or worry that contradict those bigger things. This is the only difference in terms of the time it takes for something to manifest.

Nothing is big or small for the Universe.

– The Secret Daily Teachings

FINDING A PENNY CHANGED EVERYTHING

After reading *The Secret,* I decided I'd start with something small, like the man in the book who imagined the feather. I decided to imagine a penny, and I made sure the penny in my mind was special. My penny would be heads up when I found it, it would be very shiny and new, and most importantly, it would be dated 1996. This year is very special to me, and it was very important that this be the year on the penny.

I imagined this penny four days ago, and I thought of it several times for the last few days. A few times I found myself scanning the ground in parking lots and on sidewalks, searching for the penny. I had to remind myself that I did not need to look for the penny because it would find me.

I'm not sure if I thought of the penny at all today. I had not seen any penny at all since I imagined this one. Tonight I went to the movies, and as I was leaving the theater, for some reason I glanced at the ground, and there was a shiny penny. I immediately thought it was my penny, but I made sure it was heads up before touching it. Sure enough, it was. I snatched it up and literally cried when I saw that the date was 1996!

I am so glad I decided to start small, because that was what I needed to truly believe. Now I know I can do anything and have anything, and I just want to buy this book for everyone I know! Thank you so much, I truly am so grateful!

~ *Amanda,* Connecticut, USA

It takes no time for the Universe to manifest what you want. Any time delay you experience is due to your delay in getting to the place of believing, knowing, and feeling that you already have it. It is as easy for the Universe to manifest one dollar as it is to manifest one million dollars, and the only reason why one may come faster and the other may take longer is because you thought that a million dollars was a lot of money and that one dollar was not very much. When you think something is really big, in effect you're saying to the law of attraction, "This is so big it's going to be difficult to achieve, and it's probably going to take a really long time." And you will be right, because whatever you think and feel is what you will receive. Therefore, starting with something small is an easy way to experience the law of attraction working for you. Once you've seen it at work, any doubts you might have had will disappear.

SOMETHING SMALL

I first heard about The Secret through a friend. She kept telling me that everything that happened in my life was because of The Secret. I kept thinking, *What the heck is The Secret?* She wouldn't tell me; all she said was, "If I told you, it wouldn't be a secret!" So I just kind of shrugged it off and thought nothing of it.

A few months later, my cousin from Canada visited me. In the course of conversation, we stumbled across the same topic, The Secret. He kept telling me how The Secret had changed his life and how many wonderful things had come his way by practicing it. By that time I figured, *Okay, let's see what this Secret hype is all about.* Eventually I ordered the DVD online and watched it. I thought, *Hmm . . . interesting. So what can I do to see if this works?* I figured I'd start with something very simple yet something I really wanted. It was my funny little way of trying to prove The Secret wrong.

It may seem weird, but at the time I was really craving this little Chinese dumpling called *har gow*. I was living in a mostly Caucasian community where it was hard to find an authentic Chinese restaurant. But The Secret said to visualize what I wanted, so I did. I also searched high and low to find *har gow*. I didn't mention anything about The Secret or about asking for those dumplings. I just kept thinking about it for a good week or so, but nothing was materializing for me.

Then, one night before falling asleep, I told myself, *I will eat this dish one way or another. I don't know how, but I will.* The next morning I went to work having totally forgotten what I'd said the night before. I started to do the things I normally did at work, and then my coworker came over and said, "Let's go into the kitchen; the other department has provided breakfast for everyone." I followed her in, and guess what I saw? My *har gow*! Ha-ha! Who would have thought? It was so random. And nobody eats this for breakfast! Yet it was there.

Once I truly believed, it happened! I asked the girl who had brought it in why she got it for breakfast, and all she said was, "It was the only thing open near my house at 6:00 a.m.!"

After that moment, I was a true believer in The Secret!

~ *Laarni R.*, California, USA

It's not unusual for people to "test" the power of The Secret by asking for something small "just to see if it really works." In the next story, Jason also decided to start with something really small. And he chose something so rare and specific that there could be no doubt if it manifested.

I HAD STOPPED BELIEVING, UNTIL . . .

I had been studying the law of attraction for a year before *The Secret* was released. Nothing had really worked for me, but I was excited about the movie.

When I received the movie, it was really inspiring. I watched it several times a week; I really enjoyed it!

In one section, they say that to start, "attract a cup of coffee" to you. On the audiobook, they tell the story about a man attracting a feather to him to prove the law of attraction was real.

I decided to "prove" to myself the law of attraction was real. And I wanted to do this by attracting something totally off the wall for me. I decided on a red thimble. Every day I would write that in my goal book. I would picture it, close my eyes, look at my finger, and imagine the red thimble was there. I even wrote an email to myself, very similar to what I'm writing here, telling the story I would submit once I attracted the red thimble.

Two weeks went by and nothing happened. In the movie, they said that you could attract a cup of coffee in a day, and the guy attracted the feather to himself in two days. It had been two weeks, and I had nothing!

Then one day, in an improvisation class I was taking, we were doing a skit where people had to enter and exit on a certain word. The word I was given was *thimble*.

It was a great feeling, as I could feel it was a message from the Universe saying, "Keep on doing it, it's on its way to you!"

I did, and for the next month, nothing happened.

I got discouraged, frustrated, and forgot about it. Obviously, the law of attraction did not work. Well, that's not what I believed. I believed it did work and I just did not know how to use it. Two and a half months and I couldn't even attract a thimble? I must not know what I am doing.

Then I went to a magician's convention in Las Vegas. At the end of the convention, our teacher asked us to sign his guest book and then reach inside his "treasure chest" and take out a little item he had used on the road.

Another magician signed the book and came back. "Look at this rock!" he said. "I'm going to use it as my gratitude rock!"

"Oh, you've seen *The Secret?*" I asked. He said he had. And then it hit me: My red thimble was in that treasure chest. Here was another sign. I went over, signed the guest book, opened up the chest, and right on top was a red thimble. I could not believe it! I searched through the entire box. Not another thimble in there. There was only one, and it was the color I had chosen, red.

Now, just as I told myself when I was wishing for it, I carry that thimble with me everywhere. It's in my pocket right now. Whenever I feel it, I remind myself that my belief in the law of attraction is in that red thimble. There is no way this was luck or a coincidence; it is because I created it.

I don't know why it took so long for a little thimble to come to me. I don't know yet if I completely understand how to use the law of attraction. But every time I touch that red thimble in my pocket, I am a believer. I was not a total believer, but now I am. The law of attraction is real!

~ *Jason,* Michigan, USA

Once you have personally experienced the power of The Secret and truly believe in the law of attraction, you will find that, as you put its practices to work for you, everything in your life will change for the better.

It Will Truly Change Your Life

THE SECRET CHANGED MY FAMILY'S LIFE

About a year and a half ago I was living in Los Angeles for a few months with my two little girls (a five-month-old and a five-year-old) while my husband was in South Africa. We were living apart because in South Africa we just couldn't survive financially anymore, so my husband and I had decided that it would be best if I took the girls to L.A., where I had family to help us for a while. Being apart from my husband and the girls being apart from their dad was traumatic, but I knew we all would survive.

Three different people told me about this movie called *The Secret*, and how watching it changed their lives. I went online and paid the money to watch the film. After watching it, I realized that I was actually living The Secret. I had been writing in my journal about all the things I was grateful for. I really believed that financially we would be okay, and I knew that we would see my husband again.

I also realized that when my husband and I were in the same place, something was not working, and it was because he was not living The Secret and I was. I knew that I had to get this film to my husband.

I ended up receiving a large sum of money, and I headed back to South Africa. I handed my husband the film and told him that it would change his life. At that point he had been living without his girls, on bread and water. Our dogs were starving, and he couldn't get a job or pay any of his bills. When I returned to South Africa, I had enough money to pay all the bills and buy good food, and I had the key that changed the life of our entire family.

My husband watched *The Secret* and fell asleep with it on every night for weeks and weeks. He concentrated on what he actually wanted from life instead of what he didn't have.

We wrote down on a piece of paper the life that we wanted, including the house we wanted. We cleared our life in South Africa and moved to the life we knew we wanted in Los Angeles. We have exactly the house we envisioned, our older daughter is in the best private school in Los Angeles, and my husband has not stopped working, so we have financial security. Every day of our lives we see miracles happening, miracles that are bigger than we imagined. We can see the perfection in having lived in South Africa and the time we spent apart, but now we can see a future that is glowing with white light. And it has been only a year since my husband watched the film!

The Secret has changed the lives of everyone in my family, and it will continue to do so forever! We all know now that we just have to *Ask, Believe, and we will Receive.* The more you use the tools, the faster the manifestation happens. IT IS GLORIOUS! And now, by sharing our story, we have helped change many lives around us. Thank you.

~ *Alex,* Los Angeles, California, USA

No matter where you are, no matter how difficult things might appear to be, you are always being moved toward magnificence. Always.

– The Secret Daily Teachings

Keys To the Creative Process

☞ *For the law of attraction, nothing is impossible and everything is possible.*

☞ *Whatever you consistently think about, you will attract into your life.*

☞ *Ask, Believe, Receive – just three simple steps to create what you want.*

☞ *Step one of the Creative Process is Ask. To ask, simply get clear in your mind about what you want.*

☞ *You can be as specific as you want.*

☞ *Once you have asked, know that what you want is already yours.*

☞ *Step two of the Creative Process is Believe. Act, speak, and think as if you've already received your desire.*

☞ *To believe, think, talk, and act as though you have what you want now.*

☞ *How the Universe will bring your desire to you is not your concern or your job.*

☞ *When you believe, the Universe must move all things for you to receive.*

☞ *Test the power of The Secret by asking for something small.*

☞ *Step three of the Creative Process is Receive. When you feel good, you are on the frequency of receiving, and the things you want will come to you.*

☞ *Ask once, believe you've received, and all you have to do to receive is feel good.*

☞ *Change your thoughts now, and you will change your life.*

*To change our lives, at some point
we have to decide that, rather than
suffer anymore, we are going to live
in happiness. And one way we can do
that is to make the decision to look for
things to appreciate, no matter what.*

– The Secret Daily Teachings

How I Used The Secret for Happiness

Happiness comes from giving your full attention to thoughts that make you feel happy and ignoring thoughts that don't make you feel happy.

Your life is in your hands. No matter where you are now, no matter what has happened in your life, you can begin to consciously choose your thoughts and change your life to one that is filled with happiness. There is no such thing as a hopeless situation. When you give your attention to thoughts that make you feel happy, not only will you be happy, but every single circumstance in your life will begin to change for the better!

Simply put, your current life is the result of the thoughts you have been thinking, and for that reason, your entire life will change as you begin to change your thoughts and feelings. No one knows the truth of this better than Tracy, in our next story.

THE SECRET SAVED MY LIFE!

Like so many others, I was an abused and unwanted child. Suicide, eating disorders, and other self-harm became my safety net. I carried these feelings of worthlessness and zero self-esteem into my adult life.

I threw myself into nursing, into always caring for others, as there was no one there for me. I have always had wonderful girlfriends but terrible relationships with men. My ex-husband was a serial adulterer, and my boyfriend also betrayed me. I adore my son but felt that I was not a good mother and that he deserved so much more.

At a time when suicide was a serious consideration and I simply could not see a way to keep functioning, a dear friend recommended *The Secret*. This recommendation literally saved my life. I read it, reread it, and to this day I still read a chapter daily as part of my new way of living. It took me a while to understand and to begin to learn how to live. I had to work very hard at first to change my way of thinking. But there is simply no correlation between my old life and my life today. I start each day with a smile and a prayer of thanks. I am *so* happy, and each day it is a joy to know that no one is going to take it away, because the happier I am, the more happiness I receive. I keep a daily diary as well as a vision board, and I am so grateful for all the wonderful people in my life. This includes a fabulous man who loves me so much and, as importantly, I am able to love in return. I have also learned how to love myself, which was a very difficult task. My whole life, at work and at home, is now so complete and satisfying, and I am very blessed with so much love in all areas of my life.

I have also given copies of *The Secret* to various friends of mine so that others can know just how beautiful life can be.

~ *Tracy,* Canary Islands

When you feel bad about yourself, you are blocking all the love and all the happiness that the Universe has for you. Tracy stopped entertaining thoughts of misery about herself and her past life, and she began to choose positive, happy thoughts. She discovered for herself that the happier she became, the more happiness came into her life, including her perfect partner. And this is exactly how you change your life into one filled with happiness.

Hannah, in the next story, also changed her way of thinking after she read *The Secret* and, as a result, changed her life and experienced new-found happiness.

THE BEST YEAR OF MY LIFE

I read *The Secret* when I was sort of in a rut. I didn't know where I was going in life or what I wanted to do. After I read *The Secret* at my super-boring summer job, things started to change. I started using it right away. I was totally broke at the time, but the night after reading *The Secret*, I checked my bank account, shocked to see there was more money in it than I had thought. I also envisioned something specific: a sleek silver lipstick case, and I stumbled across one a few days later.

A few weeks after reading *The Secret,* I found a new job, one that was extremely flexible and paid amazingly well. I was also offered an amazing internship at a public relations company in Manhattan.

When my junior year of college started, I was on a roll. My internship was allowing me to go to important events and meet influential and famous people. My job on the side was keeping me financially stable. My PR internship led to another internship at a major fashion magazine, where I was given fabulous free clothes and invitations to Fashion Week.

One great thing just led to another my entire year, and I am convinced that reading *The Secret* jump-started everything. My year was filled with amazing, kind people, exciting opportunities, generous gifts, glamorous parties, and most importantly, positivity! I attracted like-minded people.

I was determined to live in New York over the summer and pay rent on my own. I got hired by the PR firm where I'd interned, and I'm doing exactly what I'd envisioned for myself! So many beautiful, lucky, and inspired things happened to me this year that I wrote them all down. The list is nearing one hundred, and the good things just keep on coming!

~ *Hannah*, New York, New York, USA

Let Go of the Past

If you constantly go back over your life and focus on the difficulties from the past, you are just bringing more difficult circumstances to you now. When you think back over your life, let go of all the things you don't love about your childhood and keep only the things you love. Let go of the things you don't love about your adolescent and adult years and keep only the good things. When you do, you'll discover that you begin to feel happier and happier. The more positive thoughts you entertain, the more you notice the things that you love and that make you feel good, and the happier you become.

Like attracts like, and when you're happy, you attract happy people, circumstances, and events into your life. This is how your life changes – one happy thought at a time!

Your life is a reflection of what you hold inside you, and what you hold inside you is always under your control.

– The Secret Daily Teachings

A NEW BEGINNING!

My life began when I discovered *The Secret*.

Before *The Secret*, I was unhappy *all* the time, depressed, tried to kill myself a couple of times, always angry, and could hardly laugh. I hated myself and almost everyone around me. I used to listen to depressing music and just cry. Watch sad movies and cry. Talk about all the problems over and over again and cry. I used to drink and behave really badly toward my friends. I was really down.

Of course, things that happened in my past are unfortunately still in my life right now, but I understand that I can't change the past anyway, so it's time to move on and start living. Thanks to The Secret.

Since I started to use The Secret, I've noticed all the love that surrounds me. I can't believe I didn't see that before. Really. I'm shocked. And so happy! Everyone says I'm a different person now; I shine!

I've found some really loving friends too. Everyone just starts to show their love for me as I show mine to them. And I just get more and more of that, as I've always wanted!

My next mission was to find my soul mate. And yes, I've already found him. Do I need to tell you that he has all the qualities that I wrote down on my list?

Whenever I get a chance, I am sharing *The Secret* with people. Even if I don't know them, I just want everyone to feel what I feel. I am so grateful for this. Who knows where I would have ended up if it weren't for *The Secret*?

Thank you. And thank you, God.

~ *Micki,* Sweden

Creation means that something *new* is created – which automatically replaces the old. You don't have to think about what you want to change; instead, think about what you want to create. When you fill your life with positive thoughts and feelings, you'll find that guilt, resentment, and any negative feelings will leave you. And then you will start telling the greatest story ever told: the *real* story of your happy, amazing life.

The answer to happiness is simply to stop doing the things that are making you unhappy! And the biggest contributor not only to your own unhappiness but to that of all humanity is giving your attention to negative thoughts. The way out is to give all of yourself to positive and happy thoughts.

A LITTLE HELP FROM MY FRIEND

It was the middle of April 2008 when my best friend introduced me to *The Secret*. Her brother lives by it, and she tries to do so too. She could see I needed help. I was twenty-nine years old, on a high dose of antidepressants, and had been for four years. Social Services were monitoring my children, and I was feeling lost and alone.

I bought *The Secret*, and it immediately drew me in. Every word made sense and felt as if it were written on my heart. I read a little every night and really took it in. I started living by the rule, and the effects were immediate. I felt stronger, brighter, and more "real" than I had ever felt in my life. I stopped taking my medication and started growing stronger. I had the pills nearby in case I lost my footing, but I haven't taken them since! I am a better person, I am a truer person. I share my feelings of gratitude, strength, and belief!

Social Services closed my case last week. They said, "I cannot believe the change in you, Mel, it is as if you were a different person." I just smiled and said, "I am; I am finally me!"

I am now a very happy 35-year-old single mom to my boys, enjoying life, feeling strong, and sharing gratitude. I have my gratitude diary beside my bed and use it often. I have shared my copy of *The Secret* with several people and often remind friends who are struggling to simply look for small things to be grateful for and watch the feelings grow from there.

Sometimes I still find that I need to jog myself back onto the right path, but I am aware of that and manage to get back to happiness quickly! My Secret Shifters work, and the gratitude I feel is amazing. I have found myself in tears of gratitude over tiny things!

The Secret works! It is amazing!

~ *Melica P.*, Essex, England

The Secret Shifters that Melica refers to are things you can focus on whenever you find yourself feeling angry, frustrated, or any other negative emotion, in order to change those negative feelings in an instant. They might be beautiful memories, future events, funny moments, nature, a person you love, or your favorite music. Your Secret Shifters are unique to you, and you need to have a list of them to turn to, because different things will shift you at different times, and if one doesn't work, another will.

Like Melica, you can use Secret Shifters whenever you need to jog yourself back onto the right path. You will start to feel good, and when you are feeling good, you are powerfully attracting *good* things to you!

See It, Feel It, Receive It

Imagine what you want, really visualize having it, feel the happiness inside you, and the law of attraction will find the perfect way for you to receive it.

NEW HOUSE, NEW BABY

Since practicing the teachings of The Secret, I have manifested many things into my life: my husband, my financial stability, my health, and a new car, just to name a few.

My six-year-old daughter, husband, and I relocated to his hometown after getting married. He is the breadwinner while I focus on my education.

Recently, we decided to take the next steps in our marriage by looking to purchase our first home as well as trying for a second child. We had a time frame in mind, but as our mental deadline drew closer, we still had no house and no positive pregnancy test.

My husband is a firm believer in the law of attraction as well, and we realized that we had failed to properly Ask, Believe, and Receive!

We began constant visualization of the neighborhood we wanted to live in even though it is a high-demand area, the specific style of house we wanted, and a bottom-line price we would pay. We also began visualizing my pregnancy and our new baby. I even made a registry online of all the things we will need once our baby arrives!

We toured our prospective neighborhood daily. Desperate for the location, we ended up putting in offers on two different houses and lost to higher bids on both.

Then one night during our usual rounds of the area, we found it. The location was perfect. The style was exactly what we'd visualized. But the price was too much. We knew this would be our house, so we put in an offer anyway. The offer was so low, it was almost insulting.

We got a phone call from our Realtor the very next day. The seller had accepted our offer! This news totally blew us away, considering I also had a positive pregnancy test that same morning!

The baby registry I made prior to becoming pregnant was for a boy. I even slept with a piece of paper under my pillow on which I had written his name, gender, and eye color. And what do you know? I gave birth to a green-eyed baby boy, just as I knew I would.

It's amazing how powerful thoughts can be.

~ *Heather M.*, Buffalo, New York, USA

Have you ever started to think about something you were not happy about, and the more you thought about it, the worse it seemed? That's because as you think one sustained thought, the law of attraction immediately brings more *like* thoughts to you. But the good news is that the opposite is also true.

If you give your attention to thoughts that make you feel happy, you will attract happier thoughts. In fact, happiness is the shortcut to anything you want in your life. Just feel and be happy now! Focus on radiating out into the Universe those feelings of joy and happiness. When you do that, you will attract back to you all things that bring you joy and happiness, which will include everything you want. When you radiate those feelings of happiness, they are sent back to you as the happy circumstances of your life.

Diana, in the following story, visualized having something she really wanted, and in the end, she got even more happiness than she'd imagined.

INSTANT KARMA

When I first watched *The Secret*, it rang so true that it felt like I already knew it, but I hadn't put it all together. I have continuously experienced great things just by being grateful for everything, by envisioning what I want, and by being a careful observer.

Most recently, while taking a night flight from Boston to Phoenix, I was one of the first to board because I had paid extra for a better seat up front. On the same flight a year ago, I had been lucky enough to be the only one in my row, so I was able to stretch out and sleep during the trip. All day long I visualized the seats next to me being empty so I could enjoy the same luxury. While placing my luggage overhead, I heard an older woman behind me asking the flight attendant if she could sit in one of the front rows. It was explained to her that those seats cost more, and she quickly snapped back that she was a little claustrophobic and needed to be up front. I continued getting settled as they kindly explained that they could move her but she'd have to pay more, to which she replied harshly that she couldn't afford it.

As the rest of the passengers boarded, my delight grew as people passed but no one sat in my row. I repeated to myself how amazing visualizations can be. Finally, the attendant announced that they were ready for takeoff and requested that we all finish using our electronics before they shut the cabin door. I was happy knowing that my wish had been granted, but my mind kept flashing back to the older woman. I thought of how uncomfortable it must be for her to sit in the back feeling trapped. I couldn't possibly enjoy all this extra room knowing that she was suffering. I got up and approached the attendant who had spoken to her. I explained that I wanted to pay for the lady who was claustrophobic to be moved to a seat in my row, but that they would have to promise not to tell her I had paid for it. The attendant smiled at me and said she'd take care of it.

After several minutes, the older woman was ushered to my row and seated. We spoke only briefly, but she seemed very happy, and that filled my heart with more joy than sleep ever could. The evening seemed to fly by.

Toward the end of the flight, the attendants were going around charging each person's credit card for their food and drink. I waited for someone to stop at my row, but they seemed to have missed me. At last the attendant I had spoken to stopped at my aisle seat and leaned down near me as I held out my credit card to her. She didn't take the card. Speaking in a very soft tone, she said that she wanted to thank me on behalf of the entire crew. What I had done was the nicest thing any of them had ever experienced while flying, and they were all inspired by it. She ended by saying that not only were they not going to charge me for her seat, but they wanted to pay for my food and drink themselves.

I felt so honored and so filled with love that I could barely speak. I whispered back, "Thank you!"

It was such a wonderful and loving experience, and I'm amazed that so much joy rippled out just because I OFFERED to do something kind.

~ *Diana R.*, Phoenix, Arizona, USA

Think Happy Thoughts and Be Happy Now!

Most of us have the wrong idea about happiness. We believe that if we get everything we want, and if life continually goes our way, we will be happy. And from that belief, we create all the excuses in the world for why we can't be happy right now. "I'll be happy when I get the job, the promotion, leave this job, pass the exam, get into college, leave college, lose weight, put on weight, buy my own home, sell my home, when I'm free of debt, free of stress, free of this relationship, in a new relationship, have a family, when my health improves."

But the great revelation about happiness is that it's those very excuses that are masking your inherent happiness, which is available to you every single day, no matter what is happening in your life. It's those very excuses that are preventing you from being happy *now*. It's not the circumstances of life that are preventing you from being happy; it's the excuses you're making not to be happy! Like attracts like, happiness attracts happiness, so just drop the excuses – drop every one of them – and be happy now!

HAPPY POWER

I was one of the most miserable people I had ever known. Misery was a lifestyle for me, even though I didn't realize it at the time. Then, after more than forty years of living in utter misery, it all suddenly changed. The best part was, it was so simple. By changing just one thing in my life, I went from a severely depressed, jobless single mom who continued to turn to drinking, to operating my own independent publishing company!

I remember the first time I tried to take my life. I ran to the bathroom crying, filled with hurt. I opened the medicine cabinet and took all the prescription pills I could find and swallowed them. I just wanted to die. I don't even think I knew what the word *suicide* meant, because I was only nine years old. But I knew those pills could kill me, and I just wanted to die.

It was the first of many suicide attempts through the years. Pills, wrist-cutting, self-suffocation. Once, as a teenager, I even put a gun to my head, but my parents came home early and I threw the gun back into their nightstand and ran to my room. Starting in my twenties, I turned to alcohol. I went in and out of jobs and relationships while constantly moving. I had gone from being financially well off to being jobless, even to losing my home to foreclosure. I went from severe back pain to constantly calling in sick to breast cancer. And those were just the good times.

Then, two years ago, I finally decided to pursue my dream and become an author of psychological fiction, and I did. I poured myself into my books, which did pretty well in sales. Then one day I sat at my computer, ready to knock out my sixth book, and I didn't want to.

I was tired, exhausted, miserable. I had worked so hard at fulfilling my dream of becoming an author, and now I was right back to my emotional bottom. I couldn't believe it. I thought, *This is it*, and fell into one of my deepest depressions. I slept a lot, drank, and just felt numb. I interacted with the world as best I could but felt so removed from it at the same time. I was a single mom of two girls, and taking my life wasn't an option. So I just struggled through life as best as I could, telling loved ones what they wanted to hear because I didn't even understand the truth of the situation.

I had been studying and learning about the law of attraction for years, but something was missing and I couldn't figure it out. After a few weeks, I began to give some thought to the idea that maybe being an author wasn't what I'm supposed to do in life to make me happy. Then I said it again and again, until it narrowed down to "Make me happy, make me happy." I thought back to the dozens of times I had watched, read, and listened to *The Secret* and Rhonda Byrne saying, "You have to feel good."

Then it dawned on me. What if all I ever wanted out of everything I have been chasing was not to get the thing itself but to be happy, to feel good? What does that even mean?

I realized that I had never learned how to be happy. Sure, I had had happy moments, but happiness, no. I had been chasing it and didn't even realize it. So it was in that moment I decided I needed to learn how to be happy, and the only one who could teach me was me.

I made a list of 10 things that really made me happy and decided to start incorporating these things in my life every day. Then life got in the way and I didn't do them, but I still looked at my list every morning and gave thought to doing these things even if it was just in my mind.

And guess what happened? I began to feel happy. It was embracing every morning and proactively giving thought to things that personally made me happy that finally taught me my own happiness. Once I taught my mind and body how to be happy, I began to manifest more happy things, and because I felt happy, I naturally manifested more happy things into my life.

I wish I could go back and tell my nine-year-old self, "You don't need to take those pills to make the pain go away. You can make those awful feelings go away. You just have to make a happy list and it will be okay. It will be more than okay, it will be great." But I can't go back. All I can do now is share my story with others and tell them that after more than forty years of misery, it all changed once I became proactive in creating my own happiness, and the law of attraction did the rest. If everything I went through was to share this message with the world, it was all worth it.

~ *Heidi T.,* Chico, California, USA

Be happy *now*. Feel good *now*. That's the only thing you have to do. And if that's the only thing you get from reading this book, then you have received the greatest truth of The Secret.

We are all entirely free to choose whatever we want. The power is in your hands now, and you are the one who chooses how to use that power in your own life. You can choose:

To have a happier life today, or put it off until tomorrow.

What feels better? You choose.

– The Secret Daily Teachings

Keys To Happiness

☞ *You change your life with one happy thought at a time.*

☞ *Give your full attention to thoughts that make you feel happy, and ignore thoughts that don't make you feel happy.*

☞ *The more positive thoughts you entertain, the happier you will become.*

☞ *When you're happy, you attract happy people and happy circumstances and events into your life.*

☞ *It's not the circumstances of life that are preventing you from being happy; it's the excuses you're making not to be happy.*

☞ *Stop entertaining thoughts of misery about anything in the past. If you focus on past difficulties, you are bringing more difficult circumstances now.*

☞ *Believing negative thoughts is the biggest contributor to humanity's unhappiness.*

☞ *Fill yourself with positive thoughts and feelings, because where positivity exists, negativity cannot exist at the same time.*

☞ *Use Secret Shifters to change negative thoughts.*

☞ *To be happy, look for things to appreciate, no matter what is happening around you.*

☞ *There is no such thing as a hopeless situation.*

☞ *Practice being happy today. Your future life depends on it.*

☞ *The shortcut to a great life is to FEEL and BE HAPPY now!*

Money doesn't bring happiness –
but happiness brings money.

– The Secret Daily Teachings

How I Used The Secret to Receive Wealth

To Attract More Money, Focus on Abundance

Needing money is a powerful feeling, and so of course, through the law of attraction, you will continue to attract *needing* money. To change what you're attracting, you must tip the balance of your thoughts from lack-of-money to more-than-enough-money. Think more thoughts of abundance than of lack, and you have tipped the balance.

MONEY COMES EASILY AND FREQUENTLY!

I go to a very expensive private university where the tuition is about $40,000, not including food or living expenses. However, I come from a lower-middle-class family and receive no help from my parents, so I pay for everything myself. On the day when the school posted the financial aid packages for the following year, I got up in the morning saying, "Today will be amazing, and money comes frequently and easily." But when the awards were posted, mine was only about $5,000. I work part-time at minimum wage, and there is no way I could make up the additional $35,000 I would need for school.

Because I'd read *The Secret*, I started feeling gratitude and thanking God and the Universe for paying my school tuition. When I checked my Facebook page, I saw that a bunch of people were making negative comments about their award packages, saying things like "Bye, school," "My education is over," and "This is ridiculous and upsetting!" I just smiled and thought, *At least I'm being fully paid for!*

That afternoon I went to the financial aid office and was told that I could send them an email asking for my package to be reviewed, but it would take at least a week for them to get back to me.

I spent the rest of the afternoon asking people about scholarships and grants relating to art (which I study and create) but didn't say anything negative about my school or the amount of my scholarship. I just sought financial advice and felt gratitude and love and prayed and thanked God for helping me pay for school, saying over and over, "Money comes easily and frequently," with a smile on my face.

When I got home, I started to write my email to the financial aid office, but I wanted to double-check that my award was exactly $5,000, because I thought it might have been slightly more – maybe $5,150 or $5,200. Well, you will NEVER guess what happened when I pulled up my award on the computer. Somehow it had changed despite having been designated the "final award" earlier that day. In fact, I was being fully covered for the following year! I didn't have to pay anything at all for school and would even have some extra money to go toward paying for my apartment.

I've used The Secret before, but in the past I've also had thoughts about how I work so hard and get such good grades but am still always so broke. Now I think I can do anything and I'm a good, deserving person who can have whatever I want. This should make a believer out of anyone!

~ *Chelsea,* San Francisco, California, USA

Use Props to Help You Believe in Abundance

Using props helps you to believe that you are receiving what you asked for. You may remember that Enny talked about using a check from the Bank of the Universe in her story in the first chapter. This is one of the props The Secret Team has created to help you believe. You can download a blank check from the Bank of the Universe free of charge from www.thesecret.tv/check. The Bank of the Universe has unlimited funds for you to draw from, so you can fill out the check with your own name and whatever amount you want. Put it in a prominent place and look at it every day so you actually believe you have that money *right now.* Imagine spending the money on whatever you want. Feel how wonderful that is! Know it is yours, because when you ask and believe, it is.

Remember that the law of attraction doesn't know if you are playing make-believe or if something is real, so when you are pretending you already have what you want, you have to feel as though it is real.

When your make-believing begins to feel real, you will know that you are succeeding in bringing what you want into your reality.

– The Secret Daily Teachings

WRITE YOUR OWN CHECK

I have been a believer in The Secret from the first moment I watched the movie and have been sharing it with as many people as possible. It literally changed my life. After breaking up with my fiancé, coming close to declaring bankruptcy, and having to move back in with my parents, I figured that my life as I knew it was over. *The Secret* changed all that – in particular, the blank check available for download and printing on the website.

I have been writing "New Moon" abundance checks for years, and have seen the benefits off and on, depending on how much I believed in them. So, after watching *The Secret* and finding the blank check from the Universal Bank, I decided to print a copy and make use of it. I put in an amount that was almost impossible for me to imagine receiving: $55,000. I don't know why I chose that number, but I did. And I placed it on the corkboard that hung on the wall in my childhood bedroom, right where I could see it every night before sleep and every morning when I woke up.

Some days I'd actively work on feeling that money coming into my life, and other days I'd laugh disapprovingly at myself (which, I believe, is why it took so long).

Just when I didn't think my life could get any worse (I lost my job, my mother became dangerously ill, and the relationship with my former fiancé seemed stalled and truly doomed), I received a letter from a family member informing me that I was about to receive $50,000 in inheritance.

I honestly could not have made this up if I'd tried. I thought my entire heart was going to swell up and burst when I got that news. It allowed me to get out of debt, invest, and go back to school. Next on the list is buying an income property upon which to build my business.

~ *Mrs. Abundant,* Ottawa, Ontario, Canada

Create a Vision Board for Wealth

A vision board is a tool to help you create the image in your mind of what you want. As you look at the vision board, you are imprinting the picture of your desire in your mind. And as you focus on your vision board, it stimulates your senses and evokes a positive feeling within you. Then you have the two elements of creation – your mind and your feelings – working in full force.

– The Secret Daily Teachings

In the next story, Natalie used a vision board to help her focus on what she wanted to bring into her life. One of the things on her board was a check from the Universal Bank. As you will see, the bank gave her just what she asked for – even though, at the time, she didn't realize exactly what that was.

CHECK THE DATE

I first heard about *The Secret* back in 2009, while I was deployed to Iraq. I had just ordered a Kindle and was able to download the book from the website. I finished it in two days. Immediately, it was as if a light had been turned on in my mind. I had been praying to God to send me some answers, because I had believed that He was pure love and wanted me to live an abundant life, but nothing seemed to be working out. There had to be something I was missing, and I prayed that He would reveal it to me.

At first I attracted small things, and over time I attracted big things, like a great-paying job as a civilian, three major salary increases, and the love of my life. Once I had become comfortable attracting things, I decided to ask the Universe for the largest amount of money I could realistically imagine myself having. I sat down and asked out loud, "How much money do I really want to have?" I sat in silence for a while, and a figure just popped into my head. I knew it was the amount of money I should ask for. On New Year's 2010, I created a vision board for what I wanted to attract that year. I downloaded The Secret check from the website and filled it in. By December 31 of that same year, I had attracted every single thing on my board except the large amount of money.

I just moved the check over to the next year's board and continued mentally shopping and thinking of all the ways I would spend the money and how I would help those around me. This cycle continued for a couple of years. I would attract everything on my board except the money.

As 2012 drew to a close and we were coming up on yet another New Year, I started to look over my vision board; once again I had attracted just about everything except that large amount of money. I said to myself, "I know that the Universe will provide when I am ready to receive it." I continued saying my affirmations and meditating and reading the stories posted on The Secret website.

Now I can finally say that this New Year's Eve EVERYTHING will be coming off of my vision board, because for the first time ever I have attracted EVERY SINGLE THING that was on my board, including the very large sum of money. It was completely unexpected, and at first I thought it was some type of joke, but it wasn't. I decided to go ahead and start working on my new vision board for 2013, and when I looked at the old check, I noticed for the first time that I had written the date on it as December 31, 2012!

It must have been a typo or something, but even in my error, the Universe was obedient. I know that my "mistake" was divinely orchestrated, because if I had gotten the money when I first wanted it, I was not financially responsible, and I would have blown it. Since then I had taken control of my finances and was in a much better place to receive it.

ASK. BELIEVE. RECEIVE. The Universe is always listening and always providing. Be blessed. I know I am.

~ *Natalie F.,* Savannah, Georgia, USA

Feel Grateful in Order to Receive

When you ask the Universe for something – whether it's money or anything else – you must believe that you already have it, which means that you need to feel gratitude for having it right now. In other words, be grateful *before* you've received.

When you direct gratitude's power toward any negative condition, a *new* condition is created, eliminating the old, negative condition. This means that when you get yourself to the place where you feel grateful for money even if you don't have enough of it yet, a new condition is created, eliminating the lack of money and replacing it with more money.

AN INCREDIBLE SURPRISE

In December 2007, I urged the board of directors for the charity of which I am the executive director to purchase a building for our nonprofit. The building I found needed a lot of work, and we would have to take a new mortgage, which was making all of us very nervous, but we proceeded on faith and trust.

While we were traveling over Christmas, my wife and I were in an automobile accident and totaled our car far from home. Over the past several months, many of our friends had urged us to read *The Secret*. After our car accident, we knew we were attracting something that needed to change, so we purchased the audio version of the book and listened to it as we traveled back home. I was so excited about the concept of the Gratitude Journal that I purchased one for both of us. On January 1, 2008, on the first page, I listed all the things I already had for which I was grateful, and on the opposite page, headed Gratitude Intentions, I wrote, "I am so grateful for the $75,000 my charity received for our new building on March 31, 2008." Note that this was on January 1, so I was indicating in the present tense my gratitude for a monetary gift we hadn't yet received.

On March 15, 2008, I was contacted by a local foundation that had heard about our plans for the new building. The foundation wanted to help and asked that I arrange a meeting with my board members on March 25 to discuss the matter further. Keeping in mind that we did not solicit any help from this foundation but rather were sought out, we met on March 25 and were presented with a letter indicating that the foundation wanted to pay off the mortgage on our new building so that we could focus all our attention on our fundraising efforts. Even more astonishing, they would be making two payments: we would be receiving $75,000 on March 31, the last day of their fiscal year, and the balance on April 1, the first day of the new fiscal year!

~ *Jane G.,* Pueblo, Colorado, USA

We can never bring anything to us unless we are grateful for what we have. In fact, if somebody were completely and utterly grateful for everything, they would never have to ask for anything, because it would be given to them before they even asked.

– The Secret Daily Teachings

They say that money doesn't grow on trees, but when you're truly grateful, it may just come to you out of the blue – a gift from the Universe.

MONEY FROM HEAVEN

My boyfriend and I live in a high-rise condominium in the heart of midtown. As a result of *The Secret*, I started getting up every morning and standing on my balcony expressing gratitude for everything we have.

One morning I woke up and found a penny on our balcony. I decided to let it stay. Several months later, I woke up to find several dollar bills lying all over our balcony – seven in all. I looked around and saw that many other people had dollar bills on their balcony.

A month later, I got up very early, when it was quite dark outside, and saw what appeared to be two bills on the balcony floor. In the dark I could not tell the denomination, so I brought them inside. Lo and behold, they were two $20 bills! Wow. I was so excited that I went back outside to see if anyone else had money on their balcony. They didn't, but as I looked around, I found three more $20 bills, including one in my planter! I woke up to a total of $100 and was absolutely amazed! No one else received any money, nor was anyone missing money. What a blessing!

A week later, I had a dream in which a certain number kept showing up. Although I do not gamble or play the lottery, I mentioned to my boyfriend that we needed to play these three numbers. Such a strange statement from me! My numbers didn't come in that day, but he continued to play them for a few more days and – yup, you guessed it – the combination came in straight. Just as I'd envisioned it! I made a whopping $290.

After that I received a notification in the mail saying I was getting money in a class-action lawsuit I knew nothing about. I do not have to do anything but wait to receive it.

Without a doubt, The Secret works. Gratitude is such an integral part. I expect more will be coming any day and every day.

Blessings to all!

~ *Pat,* Georgia, USA

Imagine Having Whatever You Want

If you want to attract more money, make lists of the things you will buy with the money. Surround yourself with pictures of the things you would like and always feel the feelings of having those things now. Imagine sharing those things with the ones you love and imagine their happiness.

– The Secret Daily Teachings

Don't limit your life by thinking money is the only way to get something you want. Don't make money your only target, but make your target what you want to be, do, or have. If you want a new home, imagine and feel the joy of living in it. If you want beautiful clothes, appliances, or a car, if you want to go to college or move to another country – imagine it! All these things can come to you in an unlimited number of ways.

HOW THE SECRET MOVED US – LITERALLY

My family lived in our former home for fourteen years. We were not happy there at all. It needed many repairs and we didn't have the money to fix it, but mostly we all wanted to move away from the neighbor, who was making us all very miserable. It was a bad situation, a totally negative environment. I would rather be at work than in that house; it felt like a black hole of depression. For almost fourteen years we kept telling ourselves, "We can never move," "Nobody will ever want to buy this house," "We can't afford to move." We didn't know about the Universe's "Your wish is my command" thing, and that we were holding ourselves back with that kind of negative thinking.

We had our eye on a house that, when it first went up on the market, was way out of our league financially, but we wished for it anyway. My husband was the most determined of us all. He would point to it and say, "That is going to be our house."

We all watched *The Secret*, and our lives changed drastically for the better. All four of us used the power of The Secret together. Now we had the tools to properly visualize living in that beautiful house we dreamed of owning: picturing where our new furniture would go, looking out the window from the inside, how it would be decorated, cooking meals in the kitchen and breathing in the scent of the meal, sitting peacefully on the patio, landscaping, waving to our new neighbors from afar. Feeling the feelings. We believed we already lived there.

And within five weeks, we really did live there. We put our house on the market "as is" and received an offer of nearly our asking price within two days. The house we wanted had been on the market for eighteen months, and the price had been drastically reduced to sell. We got a mortgage quickly and without any problem and had plenty of money left over to buy new furniture. Now I can't wait to come home from work. I even come home for lunch. I thank God every day and enjoy living there every single second. We are all so happy!

~ *Gina,* Plymouth, Pennsylvania, USA

Gina and her family did something very powerful in their visualization – they used *all* of their senses. They didn't just see the home of their dreams; they felt it and even smelled it! The more senses you involve in your visualization, the more you believe what you're imagining, and the faster it will materialize.

NEGATIVE NANCY NO MORE

I have always been sort of a Negative Nancy, although I liked to look at it as being realistic. I always saw both sides of the story but always leaned toward the negative, thinking that things were "too good to be true."

From the time I was very young, I dreamed of living an adventurous life, traveling from country to country. Looking at the pictures of ancient monuments, temples, and landmarks in my school textbooks, I would think how amazing it would be to see those places with my own eyes.

Later, going to school and working office jobs, I was drained and tired. I thought, *Is this all life has to offer? Sitting in a cubicle all day long on the phone and computer?* I relished my mini-breaks when I would go outside and sit on a bench, dreaming of traveling the world. I knew in my heart that somehow it was going to happen and pictured myself working in exotic locales, globe-trotting constantly. Little did I know at the time that my wish would come true. I started reading *The Secret* and, little by little, began to practice what I was learning.

I ended up quitting my job, but after a few months, I was getting discouraged because no one was hiring anyone to travel the world. Then one day a friend, who was also unemployed, told me about a position her ex-coworker had offered her. It involved sailing on various cruise ships, doing trunk shows, and selling high-end jewelry. As soon as she finished, I said, "That is my dream job!"

A month later, I was cruising the world. What most people pay a lot of money for, I was doing for free. I stayed in passenger cabins, mingled with the guests, and wore expensive jewelry – all for work! In ports, I always had time off and traveled all over South and Central America, the Caribbean, and the Mediterranean. I finally got to see in person the very landmarks I'd discovered all those years ago in my schoolbooks. I even made it to Egypt to see the pyramids!

What really made me a believer of The Secret was when, on that cruise to Egypt, I asked the Universe to let me make a certain amount of money in commissions. I wanted it to be an odd number but one I could remember. The magic number was $5,432. Every night and day I thought of that number and pictured a check being handed to me for that amount. My commission for this particular cruise: $5,400. I've been a 100 percent believer ever since.

~ *Angie,* Fort Lauderdale, Florida, USA

Make Sure Your Actions Are in Tune with Your Desires

When you want to attract something into your life, make sure your actions don't contradict your desires. Think about what you have asked for, and make sure that your actions are mirroring what you expect to receive. Making room to receive your desires is one way of sending out that powerful signal of expectation.

HOW TO SELL A HOUSE

When I moved in with my boyfriend, I rented out my own flat, and when the tenant vacated, I decide that it was time to sell. It had increased quite a bit in value since I bought it, and my boyfriend agreed that we should put it on the market and transfer his flat into both our names.

Initially, I was certain that it would sell very quickly. I had been practicing The Secret since the beginning of the year and thought that if I wanted it enough, it would happen. The weeks went by, however, and the flat still wasn't selling. I went to The Secret website in search of inspiration. That's when it hit me – my actions weren't reflecting my desires. I wanted to sell the flat, but I wasn't actually doing anything to make it happen! I hadn't even been there since the tenant moved out, because I had started to think of it as a burden, which, of course, ensured that it would continue to be a burden.

Once I had this realization, I went round to the flat, made sure it was attractive to prospective buyers, and met with several other estate agents to verify that it was being offered at the right price.

One great tip I found on the website was to think about everything you loved about your house, thanking it, then imagining a new buyer living there happily. After reading that, I sat in the flat and thanked every room for the happy memories, explained why I was selling it, and had a very clear vision of a new buyer being very excited about living there.

Another technique that helped was to hold the keys in my hand, imagine handing them over to the new buyer, and then say as I put them away, "Thank you for the sale," and feel that I had released the flat and already sold it.

Within a few weeks of starting these practices, I received competing bids even though the market was very slow, and I actually wound up selling for more than I was expecting. As soon as I got the offer, I thought, *I really wish the buyer would want to buy the furniture as well to save us having to move it.* And what do you know, he did!

My boyfriend is now my husband, and we are currently selling our flat to move to a house because we're expecting a baby – all of which I have helped attract by using The Secret principles!

~ *Rebecca,* London, England

In the next story, the members of a band also acted in a way that reinforced their desires when they were giving a concert they feared no one would attend.

EMPTY CHAIRS

I'm in a Celtic band. We're becoming more well known, but at the time of this event, we were not. We were putting on a benefit concert in a very small town. We had teamed up with another band we hoped to perform with in the future, and we were terrified that no one would come. We had tried to perform there in the past and only four people (at the most) showed up. Also, there were several other big events in the same area on the same night. We had spent money to put on the show and had advertised it as a benefit for the fire department, so there was a lot riding on it.

One week before, we had sold only six tickets. I kept picturing a tiny audience, and I knew I had to change my thoughts immediately. I prayed for the ability to BELIEVE that people would come. I immediately had the idea to go to the small town myself to put up more posters, even though other bandmates had already plastered it all over. So on a rainy morning, I drove out there. I put up more posters but, more importantly, I infused the place with my positivity that people would come.

The day of the show, we still had only six tickets sold. We put out ninety-six chairs, and my bandmate laughed at how we'd be playing to empty chairs. I smiled and said, "We're going to need more chairs." I truly believed it.

Then, an hour before the show, people just started flocking in. We had ninety-six people there and some standing. It was a great performance, and we raised money for the fire department. It was truly magical!

~ *Kathy,* San Francisco, California, USA

When you are acting to receive from the Universe, you will feel as if you are flowing with the current. It will feel effortless. That is the feeling of inspired action and of being in the flow of the Universe and life.

Think good thoughts.

Speak good words.

Take good actions.

Three steps that will bring more to you than you can ever imagine.

– The Secret Daily Teachings

Keys To Wealth

- *You can't bring more of anything into your life by focusing on its lack. To attract more money, focus on abundance.*

- *Tip the balance of your thoughts from lack-of-money to more-than-enough-money.*

- *Make lists of things you will buy with the money.*

- *Imagine spending money on the things that you want. Tell yourself, "I can afford that."*

- *Don't make money your only target, but make your target what you want to be, do, or have.*

- *Create a vision board and fill it with images of the life you want to have.*

- *To help you believe in abundance, download a check from the Bank of the Universe (www.thesecret.tv/check).*

- *Make sure your actions are mirroring what you expect to receive.*

☞ *We can't bring anything to us unless we are grateful for what we already have.*

☞ *Gratitude is riches. Be grateful for what you want before you've received it.*

☞ *Happiness brings money.*

If you find yourself in a negative situation with someone in your life, take a few minutes each day to feel love within your heart for that person, and then send it out into the Universe. Just doing this one thing helps to remove any resentment, anger, or negativity toward that person.

Remember that feeling resentment, anger, or any negative emotion attracts it back to you. Feeling love attracts love back to you. What you are feeling for another, you are bringing to you.

– The Secret Daily Teachings

How I Used The Secret to Change Relationships

Love is the highest and most powerful emotion you can feel. Just feeling love can single-handedly transform the relationships in your life. Your ability to generate feelings of love is unlimited, and when you love, you are in complete and utter harmony with the Universe. Love everything you can. Love everyone you can. Focus only on things you love, feel love, and you will experience that love and joy coming back to you – multiplied!

Attracting the Perfect Partner

If you want to meet your perfect partner, make sure your actions are reflecting what you expect to receive. What does that mean? It means doing what you would do if you were in that relationship *now*.

FOR ALL SINGLE GIRLS OUT THERE!

At twenty-seven years old, I had been a single mother for more than three years. I was desperately lonely and really wanted to be with a good and loving partner. After attracting a few bad eggs, I gave up and continued to endure the loneliness.

Then one day I was looking for a particular street in central London when I bumped into a wedding dress shop. I was mesmerized by a dress on a mannequin in the window and went into the shop to take a closer look. The sales assistant insisted I try it on, and it fit me so beautifully that I wound up buying it. A few steps down the road, I realized I had bought a wedding dress with absolutely no reason to expect that I would be receiving a marriage proposal. I didn't even have a boyfriend and hadn't had one for years. I felt really silly.

While I continued to search for the address I was meant to go to, I was stopped by a man about my age who happened to be looking for the same address. He looked just like the actor Michael Ealy, whose picture I had on the screen saver of my computer. We continued to search for the address together, and the rest is history.

Four months later, we moved in together, and we are now married. The whole thing is surreal to me. We laugh together every day, he loves me, and I love him. Everything I ever wanted I have found in him. I just can't express how I feel in words.

I'm not asking every single girl to go buy a wedding dress when they are single, but I am asking you all to BELIEVE!

~ *Zee,* London, England

By purchasing that dress, Zee was acting *as if* she were getting married, even though, at the time, she had no idea *how* that was going to happen. Her action was saying that she *was* getting married, and as a result, the Universe delivered what she asked for – someone to marry! What action can you take that says you have already received your perfect partner?

What about making room in your closet for your perfect partner's clothes? How about setting the table for two people instead of one? Or making room in your bed by sleeping on one side instead of in the middle, and putting out two toothbrushes in the bathroom? There's no end to the creative ways you can take actions that tell the Universe you are ready to receive.

Change Your Mind to Change Your Life

In every circumstance and moment of your life, there are two paths available to you. The two paths are the positive and the negative, and YOU are the one who chooses which path you will take.

– The Secret Daily Teachings

You can change any negative situation in your life, and the way you do that is to change the way you think about it. Tammy, in the next story, had given up on believing that such a thing as true love still existed in this day and age. After reading *The Secret* and watching the movie, however, she was determined to change her way of thinking and look for the positive in everything.

NEVER GIVE UP ON LOVE

When I was introduced to *The Secret* in 2006, I was in a bad marriage and had all but given up on the idea of true love. I firmly believed that all those people I saw who claimed to be in love were just acting in public, and that the reality of their lives was probably somewhat similar to mine.

I didn't always feel that way. I grew up in a very loving home. My parents, after forty-one years of marriage, still cuddle and kiss regardless of who is watching. My grandparents on both sides were the most devoted couples I have ever seen. But I convinced myself that relationships like theirs no longer existed. Believing that was easier than admitting the truth about my own marriage.

After watching *The Secret*, I ran out and purchased the book. I was determined to do my best to change my way of thinking. I started small and reminded myself every day to see the positive side of everything. I began to write again, something I had ceased doing as my marriage went downhill. I wrote a romance story, a first for me. I wanted to see if I could write about something that I really wanted – true love – and convince myself in the process that it existed out there.

Then, as I separated from my husband and went back to school to fulfill my lifelong dream of getting a teacher's degree, my life became very busy in a most enjoyable way, and I all but forgot about the book.

About a year after that, I met a wonderful man and knew that I was falling in love. He was living in the United States and I in Canada, but as time went on, we determined to be together.

After we'd been together for a few months, I told him about the book I had started writing. I hadn't looked at it for a while and had almost forgotten the major elements of the storyline, including the names of the characters. With his encouragement, however, I dragged it out and began to read it again. My heart stopped as I realized the love interest I had given the main character (who was actually my alter ego) was the same as that of my new lover! Tears filled my eyes as I realized I had literally written him into my life.

But the story doesn't end quite there. Before I left my marriage, I had also created a vision board of places and experiences I wanted to bring into my life. The only material object on the board was the picture of a sapphire and diamond ring I had seen in a magazine. When my lover proposed to me, it was on the exact spot where my grandparents had been married sixty-six years before, and the ring he slipped on my finger was exactly the same as the one on my vision board.

Now I am living in California, soon to be married to the most wonderful man I have ever met. The Secret continues to be a guiding force for me, and I realize that all life has to offer is within my grasp as long as I believe it is.

~ *Tammy H.,* Fullerton, California, USA

The key for Tammy was writing that romance story, because in the process of writing, she completed the first two steps of the Creative Process: Asking and Believing. All that was left was the perfect timing for her to Receive the true love she had written about.

Writing or journaling is a great way to use the Creative Process – for whatever you want. If you want to attract the perfect partner into your life, you can describe in writing exactly what that person is like and what your relationship is like. You can include their likes, dislikes, tastes, hobbies, family background, and anything else important to you. You should be able to create a list of at least one hundred things that describe your perfect partner. And then just sit back and watch how the Universe orchestrates a person matching your desires into your life.

TRUE LOVE OUT OF THE BLUE!

After watching *The Secret* movie twice and reading the book,
I started applying the concepts to my everyday routine, writing
down what I wanted and being grateful. I was doing all the
right things. There was one thing, though, that I wasn't doing
right, and the Universe showed me what.

I was living in Athens when I met the perfect guy for me.
I thought he was the one. We had been together for four
months when slowly, day by day, he started disappearing on
me. In the beginning, I didn't ask him about it because I didn't
want to be pushy. Later, if a week went by without my hearing
from him, I'd ask, and his answer would be, "Don't worry; it's
nothing." Of course I would have tons of bad thoughts, but I
never got any answers. And then he disappeared completely.
No answering my calls, my texts, nothing. I would see his
car around, so I knew he was okay, and other people had
been seeing him here and there (there was no third person
involved). I was mad. I was angry. I was ready to pick up my
pieces and move back to the States.

I kept reading *The Secret*, trying to understand. And I did
finally understand. I was doing everything the book was saying
to do. That was my mistake. I was *doing* – not *feeling*. I did it all
as a checklist, like a perfect little girl. *Wrong.* You're supposed

to *feel* it. Feel what you're doing; let it be part of who you are. When my eyes were finally opened to that fact, I raised the bar. I decided that if any guy wanted to be in my life, he would have to *exceed* my standards. Period. I would never settle for anyone or anything less.

I was teaching dance at a local school. My colleagues and I often sat out on the steps to chat between lessons, and sometimes students would join us. That annoyed me because they were interrupting our conversation. So when one of them came up and said, "I'm going for some lemonade, would you like some?" I was thinking but didn't say, "No, we want you to leave."

When the student came back, he sat down next to me and started talking about trips he had taken. I didn't contribute to the conversation, but what he was saying was intriguing.

To make a long story short, on Friday (two days later), I was at a discotheque on the other side of Athens, and coincidentally, he was too (God planned it). So we danced together and talked a lot. He asked me out, I said yes. Saturday was our first date. Sunday we left for a three-day camping trip together. Today we've been together for six years, happily married for three, with a two-year-old daughter. That's The Secret.

~ *Evangelia K.,* Athens, Greece

As Evangelia discovered, when you have successfully completed the Creative Process for what you want, you cannot get in the way of the Universe delivering to you what you asked for.

You can turn your life into paradise, but the only way you can do it is to make the inside of you a paradise. There is no other way. You are the cause; your life is the effect.

– The Secret Daily Teachings

No matter how long a so-called negative relationship has gone on, and even if you can't imagine how that particular relationship could change into something positive – it can! You can change any negative relationship in your life, and the way to do that is to change the way you see the person. Look for and appreciate the positive things about the other person, and the relationship will change. You – and only you – can make it happen.

RECONCILING WITH MY FATHER

When my parents divorced, my relationship with my father changed drastically from being close and secure to filled with bitterness and anger. I lived for twenty-five years believing there was no hope of reconnecting with my dad – until my mother gave me *The Secret* DVD, and my life was changed forever.

I wept the first three times I viewed the movie. For the first time, I felt there was hope in all areas of my life. I began to visualize having a very positive relationship with my father. And then, out of the blue, my father invited me to come for a visit. We had a wonderful time rediscovering our father-daughter bond. It was a miracle I never thought possible. Now my father and I are close again and are doing great.

I cannot find the words to describe how incredible and amazing The Secret is. It turned a hopeless situation into a tremendous blessing. I hope that others around the world will discover the hope The Secret gives all of us.

~ *Amy*, Magnolia, Arkansas, USA

In the next story, Glenda was also able to discover the joy of healing a relationship with an estranged parent once she began to focus on what she loved and appreciated about her mother rather than on the differences that had come between them.

FOR MY DARLING MOTHER

All of my life, some forty-odd years, I never felt connected with my mother. When I was a teenager, we had many serious arguments, and as I got older, I just never felt I was close to her. At various points in my life, I even stopped communicating with her.

As she grew older and began to lose her eyesight, I really felt that I needed to fix our strained relationship.

After reading *The Secret*, I was writing some things about gratitude and decided to write down all the things for which I was grateful to her: the lovely dresses she sewed for me when I was a young girl, the great vegetables she grew for us all, the way she always tended to our huge garden, and so on. As I recognized these things, I felt a huge surge of gratitude for all her hard work and caring over the years.

After that, I wrote in my notebook, "I want a happy, calm, and trusting relationship with Mum." Having written that, I felt a new sense of peace about her. I hadn't actually spoken to her for about a year, and I decided to go for a visit.

When I saw her, everything between us had changed. There was no tension, no holding back. I told her about some of the difficulties I'd had in my life, and she, who had never hugged me before, offered hugs, love, and support. Never in my life had I felt this type of mother-love. It was truly a special moment in my life.

I phone Mum every week now, and we talk to each other the way I always wanted. There is just this love between us that I cannot describe in words.

~ *Glenda*, New Zealand

When you make a deliberate effort to look for things you love and appreciate more than you notice negative things, a miracle will take place. From that positive state of love and appreciation, it will appear as though the entire Universe is doing everything for you, moving every joyful thing to you, and moving every good person to you. In truth, it is.

Let Go and Live

Sometimes it's difficult to let go of negative beliefs, particularly if they're about a relationship in your life, as was the case for Sabrina.

HEALING THROUGH FORGIVENESS

I grew up a battered child; it was my mother who hurt me and my younger brother and sister. I was the eldest, so when any of us did anything wrong, I'm the one who was punished. I experienced physical and mental violence on a daily basis for the first fifteen years of my life.

When I was thirteen years old, during one of her physical attacks, my mother pressed her knee into my back to hold me down while she was hitting me. As a result, I have had a backache for many years.

Two years after that incident, I moved in with my dad and his new girlfriend. My younger sister and I were outside playing with the horses and both ended up with a hoof in our back that sent us flying into the air. One week later, my younger brother pulled back the chair I was sitting on and I fell on my back – again. My tailbone moved one and a half centimeters.

For some years, I kept going to the doctor because I couldn't understand why I still had a backache. Finally, the doctor told me that it could have something to do with the problems of the past, but also that the weight of my large breasts might be adding to the pain. Since I refused to undergo a breast reduction, I just resigned myself to having a backache.

After reading *The Secret*, I made a decision to forgive my mother and get on in my life.

Sitting on the sofa and meditating one day, I saw my mother in front of me, and I went over and gave her a hug. While I was standing with her in my arms, I told her I loved her and wanted to forgive her and let the past be past. "I now understand that you did the best you could," I told her, "with the knowledge and experience you had then." I kept saying, "I love you and forgive you." I began to cry and let the tears fall down my cheeks. I sat in the meditation for a long time and just forgave. I was saying, "I love you and let the little Sabrina inside of me cry all she wants." It was one of the scariest yet most beautiful things that had ever happened to me.

After having that experience, I told my dad and stepmom that I had forgiven my mother and let the past be past. That night my backache went away and has never returned. The only thing I did to make it go away was to forgive my mother.

~ *Sabrina,* Denmark

Sabrina's use of visualization and meditation made it possible for her to begin thinking positively about her mother, which helped her not only to let go of any emotional pain from their past relationship but also to overcome the physical pain in her body. When you change the way you think about a situation, everything connected to that situation will change.

The More You Give, the More You Receive

Giving opens up the door to receiving.

Give kind words. Give a smile. Give appreciation and love.

There are so many opportunities for you to give and thereby open the door to receiving.

– The Secret Daily Teachings

THE GIFT

I began reading *The Secret* in the airport the night I was returning home from a business trip. On the plane, I'd reached the section where readers are urged to imagine themselves driving the car of their dreams. I tried to envision the steering wheel with the emblem of the Jaguar, but a Porsche emblem kept appearing in my mind. Finally, I realized that the car I kept visualizing was the Porsche my husband always dreamed of owning.

I created it in my mind clearly: its color both inside and out; its perfectly preserved exterior and interior; its highly maintained mechanics. I knew that the car we could afford was a 1997 model. At the time that would have made it ten years old. I also knew that most cars with so many years under their seat belts would be more than showing their age. Yet I continued to envision this decade-old car as if it were brand-new, straight down to the mileage.

As I was envisioning all this, I found myself thinking of something I wanted much more – a renewed relationship with my son-in-law, Brandon. Tension and distance had come between us as my daughter's dream wedding turned into a very rocky marriage. As a result, he and I had barely spoken in more than five months.

I told myself that I wanted an opportunity to meet with him alone, not to discuss their marriage but simply to listen and let him know I cared for him very much and believed in his ability to succeed.

As the plane landed, I was so excited about what I'd read in *The Secret* that I couldn't wait to share it with my husband.

The next morning, I took my daughter and nephew out to breakfast. In the restaurant, my daughter got a call on her cell phone, and looking very surprised, she handed me the phone and said, "It's Brandon. He wants to talk to you."

Brandon, who a month before had taken a sales position with a local car dealer, told me he remembered that Ted, my husband, once said he'd love to have a Porsche Boxster. Then he excitedly began to describe this very unusual car that had arrived on his lot just that morning. There had been only one previous owner, who'd been very meticulous and driven it no more than a couple of blocks a day for the last ten years. Brandon used the term *showroom perfect* as he described this car that was just as I'd created it in my mind the night before. Needless to say, I told him not to let anyone near it, and I'd be right there.

When I arrived, it was truly *the* car – the color, showroom perfect, with fewer than 5,000 miles on it! I told him that I'd have to show it to Ted, who I was sure would be delighted, and Brandon said he was sure that would not be a problem as he asked for my driver's license and went to get the keys.

When he returned, he reported that his manager had only one stipulation: Brandon would have to accompany me on the two-and-a-half-hour trip to and from my husband's restaurant.

I was truly amazed: Both my requests had been manifested in less than twenty-four hours. My husband was receiving the car of his dreams, and on that drive to the restaurant, Brandon and I were healing a relationship that was very important to both of us.

Since that night on the airplane, I have given copies of the book to our dearest friends; we are filling our Gratitude Journals daily, and Brandon has the audio in his car as I write.

~ *Durelle P.,* Dallas, Texas, USA

Joy attracts more joy. Happiness attracts more happiness. Peace attracts more peace. Gratitude attracts more gratitude. Kindness attracts more kindness. Love attracts more love.

– The Secret Daily Teachings

Keys To Relationships

☞ *You can change any so-called negative relationship by changing the way you see that person.*

☞ *Look for the things you love and appreciate about the other person, and the relationship will change.*

☞ *As with everything in life, when it comes to relationships, you need to believe you already have what you want in order to receive it.*

☞ *When trying to attract or restore a relationship, make sure your actions reflect what you expect to receive.*

☞ *To attract the perfect partner into your life, envision every detail of what that person is like and write it all down.*

☞ *What you are feeling for another, you are bringing to you.*

☞ *Feeling love can single-handedly transform the relationships in your life.*

☞ *Love everything you can. Love everyone you can. Focus only on things you love.*

☞ *The more you give, the more you'll receive in your relationships and in your life.*

The law of attraction is a powerful tool to summon the healing power within us, and can be used as an aid in total harmony with all of the wonderful medical procedures that are available today.

– The Secret Daily Teachings

How I Used The Secret for Health

I know that nothing is incurable. At some point in time, every so-called incurable disease has been cured. In my mind and in the world I create, "incurable" does not exist. Since the film *The Secret* was released, we have been inundated with miracle stories of all types of diseases dissolving from people's bodies after they put The Secret into practice. All things are possible when you believe.

Change Your Mind, Change Your Health

DOCTORS SAY IT'S A MIRACLE

At twenty-four I was diagnosed with a mysterious, life-threatening heart condition. In fact, I was told that the chances of having this condition were one in a million. I was put on a couple of medications and had a defibrillator implanted in my chest. The thought of death was my daily companion.

Five years later, after a divorce and two failed heart surgeries, I began searching for answers. After watching *The Secret* and putting it into practice, I began a spiritual journey of discovery to figure out why I had this heart condition. It took a couple of years, but finally, I gained a new appreciation of life and no longer felt the need to harbor this condition. I decided to let it go.

I would tell myself, *One day you are going to wake up and discover that you do not need your meds anymore.* About six months later, I awoke one morning and threw on my tennis shoes to go to the farmers' market. I was almost there when I realized I had forgotten to take my heart meds. A voice in my head said clearly, "Today is the day! You don't need to take them anymore."

I have not taken any medication since then, and I had the defibrillator removed six months ago.

Initially, the doctors hesitated to remove the device because there was no medical proof of how the condition was reversed, but neither could they find any proof that the condition still existed. They said it was a miracle and that there were *no* other documented cases of anything like this ever happening.

~ *Knight H.*, Colorado Springs, Colorado, USA

Naturally, any decision to discontinue prescribed medication or treatment should be made in consultation with a medical professional. But what this person and her doctors were able to achieve together demonstrates the power of the law of attraction when used in conjunction with traditional medicine.

Beliefs are simply repeated thoughts with strong feelings attached to them. A belief is when you have made up your mind, the verdict is in, you've nailed the door shut and thrown away the key, and there is no room for negotiation.

If you've developed negative beliefs about your health, go back to the negotiation table. It's never too late to change your mind, which is essential if you want to change your health.

MY MIRACLE HEART

I received a call from a stranger about my inheritance. That's how I found out about my father's sudden death. He was fifty-three, and he died of an aortic aneurism from a rare genetic disease called Marfan syndrome. I went to the chief of cardiology at Cedars-Sinai in Beverly Hills and found out that I had Marfan syndrome too.

Marfan syndrome is a genetic condition for which there is no cure; it often results in death from an aortic aneurism. It can strike people early in life, usually in their twenties. I was twenty-eight.

I was devastated. I had a first-degree heart block and a heart murmur. I would need a pacemaker as the heart block progressed to the second degree, but the real concern was my aortic valve and the possibility of a rupture. I wouldn't be able to have children. I had always been extremely athletic in competitive sports, from volleyball to swim teams to college tennis. I was completely into nutrition and fitness. After the news, I was truly terrified. Where I used to view myself as strong and positive, I now saw myself as weak and fragile, with what I was told was a "ticking time bomb" in my chest. While I tried to stay my usual positive self, in the back of my mind I was always aware of the imminent danger and my inescapable mortality.

I lived with this fear, getting checked by my cardiologist twice a year for years, until I saw *The Secret*. I was due for another visit to the cardiologist right around that time. I was awestruck by the man who healed himself from the plane crash. I decided right then and there that I was going to heal my heart. I believed it and knew it was possible.

I quickly banished any negative thoughts about my heart and refused to let them enter my mind anymore. Every night as I lay down in my bed, I placed my right hand on my heart, and I visualized a strong heart. I rehearsed in my mind my heart beating strong, looking and sounding the way a strong healthy heart was supposed to. Every morning when I woke up, I said, "Thank you for my strong, healthy heart." I visualized the cardiologist telling me that I was cured. I didn't tell anyone what I was doing for fear of judgment or disbelief. I postponed my cardiologist appointment for about four months to give myself enough time to try this.

I went to the cardiologist with my medical file full of past electrocardiograms and echocardiograms confirming my physical heart problems. Nervous and excited, I tried to calm myself as I got hooked up to the EKG and then had the sonogram.

The cardiologist came in with the test results, completely dumbfounded. There was *no* sign of a first-degree heart block. There was *no* heart murmur. There was *no* expansion in my aorta. He checked and rechecked the old tests and the new one that showed a perfectly healthy heart with no physical symptoms of Marfan syndrome! He had no explanation. I was ecstatic, but honestly, I was not surprised. It was exactly as I had envisioned. I literally *ran* out of the cardiologist's office across the lot to my car, feeling stronger and more alive than I ever have in my life.

I called my mom, whom I had previously bought a copy of *The Secret*, and told her how I had used its practices and now had a healthy, strong, normal heart. I'd never heard her cry so hard!

~ *Lauren T.,* Laguna Beach, California, USA

Allow the doctors you have chosen to do their work, and keep your mind focused on well-being.

Think thoughts of well-being. Speak words of well-being. And imagine yourself completely well.

– The Secret Daily Teachings

One Small Positive Thought at a Time

All stress begins with one negative thought. One thought goes unchecked, and then more thoughts come, and more, until stress manifests. The effect is stress, but the cause was negative thinking, and it all began with one little negative thought. No matter what you might have manifested, you can change it . . . with one small, positive thought and then another.

BEAUTIFUL HEALING

Since I listened to the CD of *The Secret,* many amazing things have occurred in my life, but none more so than my healing of the ulcerative colitis that had plagued me for years.

Born and raised in a Pentecostal-type home, I grew up a very anxious child, terrified of hell and the return of Christ. In my heart, I questioned the Church. If God is love, like the Bible teaches, then why am I feeling so much fear? I was scared of everything.

My dad had ulcerative colitis, and my mom told me that if I continued to worry about needless things, I too would get it. At the age of twenty-three, I was, indeed, diagnosed with ulcerative colitis.

I stopped dreaming and singing and started drinking heavily in my late twenties, when I settled into a relationship that was "good enough." It was then that the ulcerative colitis really began to flare up.

Even after I left Mr. Good Enough and stumbled upon my "Made for Me" man, my gut continued to cramp and bleed daily. By then I was working full-time and single-handedly raising my young daughter and troubled teen son. My brilliant love affair made all the pain bearable, but my body was getting tired.

I lost my job, and with the love and care of my then-new husband, I was able to focus purely on healing my past and my body. Bleeding daily, I was badly anemic and very tired. Mentally, I was pretty beat up too. I visited a specialist, who told me that I would be on a high dose of prescription anti-inflammatories and would require periodic enemas for the rest of my life. Dejected and hopeless, I filled my body with medication and just dealt with it.

More than a year later, I was still bleeding almost every day. In every other way, I had a brilliant, perfect life, but I still felt physically and emotionally horrible. After a big debate with myself, I bought *The Secret*. Five minutes into the book, tears of joy were streaming down my face. I could not believe how my unspoken beliefs were now being confirmed.

That day my life changed. The colitis symptoms immediately let up. I Google Image–searched a healthy colon and would visualize that in me. I gave thanks for my healing and blessed my body continuously. I imagined water being healing for my body. I figured that our bodies are made up mostly of water and that adding to it would be beneficial, flushing out any unhealthy bacteria. So, I would drink water and give thanks. (It was only later, after listening to *The Power*, that I learned how water reacts to a positive environment.)

I continued to listen to *The Secret* daily. My body was healing and I was feeling the best I had ever felt in my life, and yet my health was still not where I wanted it to be.

Mentally, I struggled with letting go of my past and dealing with confrontations with loved ones. I had bouts of anxiety and was very frustrated that I could not be "calm and cool." I was very hard on myself. I had all the tools and was getting everything I wanted. Why wasn't my health perfect? I knew that I was so close to achieving full health, but I was still missing something.

After six months of listening to *The Secret* every day and reading books on spiritual growth and healing and gratitude, I bought *The Power* and discovered what I'd been missing. What I'd forgotten to put first before everything else was love. I instantly allowed myself to love everything, from the smallest to the biggest. Two days later, the colitis symptoms were gone.

I now start my days feeling love. I picture my family and friends and I give them love. I picture them happy and successful. I am blown away by how the Universe has reacted. Confrontations have cleared up. People around me became happier. I'm not doing anything more than imagining and feeling love. It is so easy to do. I now let myself feel love for everything! I give love to everything and everyone.

My biggest thing was finding the love in my past. If a memory comes up that causes me grief, I just find something I loved about that time and allow myself to feel it. Then that moment in time doesn't ever bother me again.

Every area of my life is better than it's ever been. The Secret opened the door to a brand-new way of thinking and life for me. On my birthday, two and a half years after I first listened to *The Secret,* the results of my biannual test showed that the ulcerative colitis I'd been plagued with for so many years was no longer there. All that remains is scar tissue. I am the healthiest and happiest I have ever been in my life.

~ *Jessica C.,* Vancouver, British Columbia, Canada

You cannot bring what you want to you if you are feeling stress. Stress or any tension at all is something you have to remove from your system.

The emotion of stress is saying strongly that you do NOT have what you want. Stress or tension is the absence of faith, and so to remove it, all you have to do is increase your faith!

– The Secret Daily Teachings

HOW THE SECRET EXPANDED MY LIFE

I have suffered from agoraphobia, anxiety disorder, and panic disorder most of my adult life and had basically given up on ever doing anything out of my comfort zone until I read *The Secret* and started to become very positive about everything.

I started with positive affirmations every day. Then I stopped talking about what I couldn't do and just spoke about what I could do.

Finally, after thirty-three years of never getting on a plane or going overseas, I took my nine- and twelve-year-old sons on a two-week trip to Bali.

I went from being someone who could not even go into the local shopping center to being a world traveler. And it's all thanks to The Secret!

~ *Karen C.*, Sydney, Australia

As Karen's story shows, affirmations can help overcome fear and anxiety, and even panic disorders.

The effective use of affirmations depends entirely on how much you believe them when you say them. If there is no belief, then the affirmation is just words that have no power. Belief adds power to your words.

— **The Secret Daily Teachings**

There Is Nothing More Important Than Feeling Good

Being healthy means having a healthy body *and* a healthy mind. You can't be happy or healthy if your mind is full of negative thoughts or negative beliefs. If you can keep your mind healthy, you will help the health of your body.

One way to keep your mind healthy is to simply not believe negative thoughts. No matter what is going on in your life, turn your mind to positive thoughts of beauty, love, gratitude, and joy, and you will give your body the panacea it needs.

WAKE-UP CALL

My life has always been about health. For nearly forty years, I have practiced deep meditation, exercised, eaten the "right" foods, and gotten eight hours of sleep. Therefore, it was quite a shock for me and my doctor when I was diagnosed with breast cancer one week before my sixtieth birthday.

For the next several days, I lived with the paralyzing fear that often follows such a diagnosis. And then, somehow "coincidentally," I saw a newspaper article about *The Secret*. I sent for the audio CDs and listened – in the car, going to bed, while walking the dog. I realized that working all the time and not enjoying life, as my husband and I had been doing, was *not* something to be proud of, so we sat down and reprioritized our lives to create more balance.

The next thing I did was to return all the books on cancer that well-meaning friends had given me, and to stop searching on Med.com. I needed to stop identifying with breast cancer patients. Instead, on my daily walks, I started saying out loud, "I am filled with radiant health! Thank you, thank you, thank you!" In the shower, I imagined all my cells in perfect harmony, all systems integrated, all tissue healthy. I gave thanks for everything, all day – from the time I woke until I went to bed, repeating over and over how healthy I was.

I knew I needed about six weeks for this to work, and the hospital had said they would call to schedule my surgery in a few days, so I also used The Secret to create more time for healing. I repeated, "I have all the time I need to heal," and the Universe listened! No one called, and after five and a half weeks, I finally called the hospital myself. Would you believe, someone had lost my paperwork!

But by that time, I could hardly feel any lump!

After my surgery, the doctor told my husband that it had been difficult for her because she couldn't find the tumor and kept sending additional tissue to pathology to make sure she had the right spot! *No one* could explain why the tumor had shrunk so much. But I can!

I now live life enjoying every minute, and though I wouldn't want to go through any of this again, I am so much happier for having learned the power of thoughts and the wonderful choices we get to make about our lives.

~ *Carol S.*, Syracuse, New York, USA

Healing through the mind can work harmoniously with medicine, as Carol discovered. When you undergo any test or treatment, imagine the outcome you want and feel that you have already received that outcome. When Carol went through with her surgery, she had already used The Secret to establish her total belief in a positive outcome – and that's just what the Universe delivered.

The impact of stress and negative thoughts on our physical body over a sustained period of time results in disease. We can change negative thoughts through two different approaches. We can choose to flood our body with positive thoughts and affirmations about health, which prevents negative thoughts from existing at the same time. Or we can choose not to identify with negative thoughts. When we don't give any attention to negative thoughts, they are depleted of energy and will dissolve immediately. Both approaches work, and both approaches involve not giving any attention to what you *don't* want. And isn't that The Secret, after all?

In the next story, Tina knew that her negative thoughts had to go if she was to attract the health that she wanted.

I BECAME INVINCIBLE

I was thirty-two years old and recently divorced when I was diagnosed with early menopause. I still remember my doctor trying to calm me down as he mumbled to himself, "This is the youngest I've ever seen." I was in tears for days, weeks, months, knowing I would never be a mother. It was devastating. No words can describe the pain and the journey I went through. There was no cure, and there was no recommendation from the doctor. Trust me, I traveled around the world trying to find a cure, a reason, a way to turn back time and bring back my normal, regular menstrual cycle. I tried herbal pills, acupuncture, birth control pills, hormone therapy. You name it, I've been through it.

The truth is, deep down I wasn't surprised. I've always been a very negative person. Before I was given the news, I had heard stories of women in their early thirties diagnosed with menopause, and I'd always worried that it would happen to me. Golden rule of The Secret: if you worry about something, it will happen to you.

After five years of trying one medication and doctor after another, I had something worse happen. I developed high blood pressure and calcium deficiency because I was aging rapidly. My kneecaps were constantly in pain when I walked too much. And I had to start taking blood pressure medication. I was only thirty-six, but I felt as if I were sixty-three. In fact, I woke up every morning thinking that I would probably die very young. I was depressed every single day.

I got married again, and my husband was very patient with my emotional ups and downs. He encouraged me to go out, exercise, and eat a healthy diet. At a certain point, I decided to stop all the hormone pills just to give my body a break.

One day after I had stopped all the hormones, I walked into the bookstore and saw *The Power*. I'd read *The Secret* before but told myself there was no point in following it because I was such a negative person. But somehow a strong voice was telling me that this book would be my only hope and only cure. And if none of the treatments was working, perhaps I should be my own doctor and treat myself a different way.

I read the book and was immediately hooked. I bought the audiobook and listened to it every day – on the subway, buying groceries, walking on the street, when I woke up on sleepless nights. I was in tears every time I heard that I should be able to do anything and get anything I wanted in life.

Then I began to practice positive thinking and imagination. I imagined myself having regular and strong blood vessels. I imagined myself taking no medication and still having normal, healthy blood pressure. I imagined myself running around without feeling any pain in my knees. And I imagined myself having a normal menstrual cycle. I felt love every single moment for the very first time in my life. I no longer felt depressed about little things. I felt blessed and happy to be surrounded by people I loved and places I enjoyed.

After three months, I stopped taking all my medications. After several more months without any medication, my blood pressure was normal. My knees were no longer in pain, and most unbelievable of all, I got my period.

My thanks to the entire team from *The Secret* for giving me the strength to overcome the challenges in life. You made me believe that I am strong, I deserve everything, and I am Invincible.

~ *Tina,* Hong Kong

Isn't it amazing to know that to improve your health, you simply turn your mind toward health? Let positive thoughts sweep you away. Let positive pictures of health fill your mind and body. Let feeling good and joyful be your focus, and as you turn toward these feelings, know that you have turned away from their opposites.

Receiving the Gift of Life

We have received many stories from women who had lost all hope of having a child, but after reading *The Secret* and putting its principles into practice, they were able to conceive. I believe that what these stories indicate is that there are no "hopeless" cases and that using the practices in *The Secret* can create positive outcomes in every situation.

BLESSED WITH MY SWEET BABY GIRL

My story begins when I got married to the love of my life. Our priority was to settle down first and then bring a child into our lives.

When we tried to have a baby, however, somehow things did not work out. So we decided to visit the doctor, who advised us to take certain tests. We went through a lot of medical treatments but were unable to find the reason for not conceiving.

Our parents, relatives, neighbors, and friends were asking for the news of a baby, and we had nothing to report. My married friends were being blessed with children, and there I was with tears in my eyes, praying for my little angel. I was very depressed and anxious.

One day my doctor said that if I didn't conceive by the end of the year, I would have to start IVF treatment. That was devastating news. The treatment was very expensive, and there was no assurance that it would succeed on the first attempt. Then one of my close friends insisted I consult an astrologist, whose advice might be helpful.

My husband and I made an appointment, and that meeting changed my life. We explained our health problem to the astrologist, who asked me if I had watched *The Secret*. I said I had. In fact, I had seen it several years before. "So," the astrologist said, "if you already know The Secret, why are you coming to me with your problem? You can solve it on your own." He guided us on how to use The Secret, and on that very day, I promised myself that I had the right to conceive naturally.

From then on, my husband and I incorporated The Secret into our routine.

First I bought the book and read it carefully. After reading it, I thanked God whenever I saw a pregnant woman, for the very sight of her. I started buying clothes for my baby girl. I collected pictures of the baby's growth and saved them on my cell phone. I started using baby soap. I made a place for my child's clothes in my cupboard. Each day my husband and I thanked God for our cute angel. Whenever my relatives asked me about good news, I told them, "Very soon," with a smile on my face. I was doing this as if our little angel had already arrived.

Nine months after starting to practice The Secret, I took a home pregnancy test that came out positive. I had conceived without any medical intervention.

I had tears rolling down my cheeks! I was super-happy. My husband was happy too, that I had conceived without any medical treatment. My entire pregnancy went very smoothly, and nine months later, we were blessed with a sweet and healthy baby girl. Many people had been telling me it would be a boy, but I knew even before conceiving that I would be blessed with a baby girl.

So, to anyone who is having trouble conceiving, I just want to say, never lose hope and be positive. Just ask the Universe and believe that you have already received and you will be blessed with everything you wish for!

~ *Samita P.*, Mumbai, India

When Samita was feeling gratitude for other women's pregnancies, she was feeling good about pregnancy, even though she was not yet pregnant herself. Whatever you are grateful for – whatever you feel good about – you bring to you.

In addition to being grateful and thanking the Universe for the baby girl she *knew* she would conceive, Samita included two more extremely important steps in her daily routine. She thanked God for every pregnant woman she saw, and she cleared space in her closet and began to buy clothes for the baby.

Samita's actions of making room in the closet and buying clothes for her daughter helped her believe not only that she was going to have a baby but also that a baby was coming *now*! It's been said that the Universe abhors a vacuum and will fill it immediately; you can see that in Samita's case, that's exactly what happened.

The things that come most quickly into your life are the things that you BELIEVE in the most. You can bring to you only what you BELIEVE, so you must BELIEVE to receive what you want.

– The Secret Daily Teachings

In the next story, Andrea wanted to manifest not just one but *two* much-wished-for pregnancies by using props and the power of visualization.

THE POWER OF VISION

It was the summer of 2003. I was on holiday, sitting on a golden sand beach with the sun shining when my mother told me the amazing news that she was pregnant with her sixth child. We both adored children and couldn't wait to have a new baby around the house, as the youngest was now eleven.

However, three months later, at her first scan, our world crashed around us. The baby's heartbeat was not there, and my mam had miscarried. We were devastated.

Over Christmas 2004, our dreams and nightmares were relived. My mam became pregnant again only to lose the baby at four months. The doctors said that at forty-two, she was too old and her eggs were not strong enough. We had given up hope and accepted the fact that we would never have another baby in the house.

Two years passed with both of us still yearning for that baby. Then *The Secret* came into our lives. At first I was a skeptic.

Then my mother made me watch the DVD. After the first five minutes I was glued – something in my heart and mind just clicked, and for weeks I couldn't stop smiling.

A few weeks later, I started to visualize. I got out an old doll I had for years, and every night before bed, I would lie holding it for ten to fifteen minutes and visualize my baby sister or brother in my arms, the baby's heart beating against mine, their warmth and love embracing me. I also wrote on my calendar that on August 14, 2007, my seventeenth birthday, I would hold my real brother or sister. I didn't know it, but my mother had written on her calendar that on my father's fiftieth birthday, in September 2007, she would have her sixth child.

Just months after starting to visualize, I sat with a miracle in my arms. With her heart beating against mine, and her warm face snuggled into my cheek. My baby sister was and still is beyond beautiful, beyond perfect, and beyond belief. She is faith, hope, and love; she is the miracle of life.

Yet another story from my life shows how powerful The Secret truly is. At the age of twenty, I was diagnosed with some fertility issues. I was busy running my business, which I had opened at the age of eighteen, thanks to the information I had learned from *The Secret*. The diagnosis devastated me;

I had always wanted to be a mother. I focused on my business, but a couple of years later, a lot of signs were coming into my life. I was diagnosed with further problems. I had to take action! So I began investigating my options and continued being grateful for my life and having the opportunity to love and teach so many wonderful children. I truly believed that I would find the right path. I began visualizing being pregnant and having a little baby (one that I didn't have to hand back at the end of the day). The path that began to appear was different from those more traveled, but I knew it was the one for me.

I decided to go for fertility treatment and try to conceive. It was a difficult road and even harder traveling it alone. There were many obstacles and heartaches, but I knew I could see the light at the end of the tunnel. I kept visualizing and staying positive, but I was experiencing something strange. When I tried to envision my future with a child, I couldn't. My mind kept seeing two. Everywhere I went, I started to see twins. When I visualized, I saw twins. I tried to ignore it, but it was such a strong image in my mind that I decided to focus my visualization on twins. I placed a picture of twins on my vision board and I kept moving forward on my path to my dream. My heart thumped when I got the news that my second round of treatment was a success and I was pregnant, but the best news of all came at my eight-week scan. IT WAS TWINS!

I couldn't believe it. Everything I had imagined over the past few months was coming true before my eyes. I was not only going to be a mother but a mother of twins. Now every single moment I spend with my boys is filled with an overwhelming sense of gratitude and love. I am so thankful that I have been blessed with a true understanding that *what you believe you can achieve.*

~ *Andrea,* Ireland

The reason visualization is so powerful is because, as you create pictures in your mind of seeing yourself with what it is you want, you are generating thoughts and feelings of having it now. You are emitting that powerful signal out into the Universe, and the law of attraction will take hold of that powerful signal and return those pictures to you as your life circumstances, just as you saw them in your mind.

How can it be that the mind has so much power to change physical things? Ancient traditions tell us emphatically that everything – absolutely everything – we perceive in the physical world is made of "mind." They say that all matter is actually "mind stuff," and that is why the mind can change anything.

Healing Your Child

Sometimes life can throw us a real challenge, and for parents, the ultimate challenge can be when their child's health appears to be in real danger. The parents whose stories I am about to share decided to use the wisdom of The Secret to try to heal their child in the same way they would heal themselves.

BROUGHT BACK TO LIFE

I had been given *The Secret* a few years earlier by a friend, and it sat in the cupboard as a must-read-one-day. I did start it one day but was distracted by one of my three kids. Later that night, I was on the Internet and came across *The Secret* again. Within days, I had read the book all the way through for the first time, watched the DVD with my husband, and started to write in my Gratitude Diary. I had turned myself from "It will never happen to me" to "It is all going to be mine."

Two weeks later, my husband left for China on business. My youngest son, Liam, just seven weeks old at the time, had been born prematurely with pneumonia and had not been well. Two days later, he was up all night and then started losing color, so I rushed him to the hospital. By the time we got there, he had stopped breathing. He was in a very bad way, and a lumbar puncture confirmed that he had bacterial meningitis.

In the hours that followed, Liam's heart stopped beating four times, and each time he had to be brought back to life. At that point the doctor told me that he was gravely ill and I should call my husband to come home.

It should have been an awful time and I should have been hysterical. But I remained calm throughout and believed that my son would be home and well very soon. I sat in the hospital with my mother on the first night, waiting for my husband to come back and listing all the things for which I was grateful:

I was grateful for my fast action in getting to the hospital.

I was grateful for the excellent staff looking after my son.

I was grateful for my friends who helped with support while my husband was on the fifteen-hour flight from China.

I never thought of the bad, just of the positive, and it made me stronger. In fact, as my inner strength increased, so did my son's health. I would post daily updates on Facebook, and instead of saying how bad Liam was, I wrote about only the good things that had happened that day and what I was grateful for. At the end of each post I would write "THE SECRET."

Finally, the day came when Liam was well enough to go home, and the staff told me they were shocked to see him leaving the hospital in such happy circumstances. They had been convinced he wouldn't make it through the first night and were amazed at how calm I had been. One of the doctors asked, "Is the book I always see you holding a Bible?" I told him why I was so calm, what I believed, and that the well-worn red book that had lost its paper cover was called *The Secret*.

I still practice. Normally, I just finish each night with a quick note on my iPhone's notepad, thanking myself for the amazing day and looking forward to the next day. But I also write in my Gratitude Diary.

My mum used to say to me, "You want the fairy tale, Becky, and the fairy tale does not and never will be real," and I pretended to believe her. But each night when I went to bed, I would put myself to sleep thinking about all the wonderful things that would happen to me. I've received most of what I've asked for, but there have also been some difficult times, and I never understood until I read *The Secret* that I had brought both the good and the bad into my life.

The new me is on top of the world and can do anything, because obstacles are a thing of the past.

~ *Rebecca D.,* Birmingham, England

Gratitude, faith, and unwavering optimism were the keys to Rebecca healing her baby boy. Even when Liam was at his sickest, she never stopped being grateful.

You will have heard people say to count your blessings, and when you think about the things you're grateful for, that's exactly what you're doing. It is one of the most powerful practices you can ever do, and it will turn your whole life around!

To experience deep gratitude, sit down and write a list of the things you are grateful for. Keep writing your list until your eyes are overflowing with tears. As the tears come, you will feel the most beautiful feeling around your heart and all through the inside of you. This is the feeling of true gratitude.

– The Secret Daily Teachings

PREGNANCY COMPLICATIONS
WITH A HAPPY ENDING

In January 2013, I had a positive pregnancy test. I already had a beautiful baby girl, and my husband and I couldn't wait to add to our family.

My pregnancy was going perfectly. I had my twelve-week scan, and all appeared to be well with our baby. At my twenty-week scan, however, that all changed. The sonographer noticed quite a large lump on top of the baby's head. I could see by the technicians' faces that it wasn't good news. Within twenty-four hours, I was on my way to a specialist for the diagnosis.

I had another scan, and the doctor explained that the lump on the baby's head was a fluid-filled sac and there was a real concern that it could put pressure on the brain, which could cause our unborn child to have a severe disability. I was already feeling my baby move and kick. I never imagined that I would be in this situation. The doctor told me that the baby would definitely have some kind of disability, but he could not tell me at this stage how severe it would be. The possibilities included the baby being born blind, deaf, and unable to speak. Only time would tell how badly the brain would be affected as the pregnancy progressed. I was offered a termination then and there, and I was told that most people in my position would choose to terminate the pregnancy because many felt that they could not cope with "waiting to see" how things worked out.

At that point there was nothing wrong with my child, and her brain was healthy. I had my cry and decided that I would use what I had learned from reading *The Secret* to ensure that I gave birth to a healthy baby. I told the doctors that I would be continuing with my pregnancy.

After being offered a termination and then leaving the doctor's office, I was walking down the street with my husband when a postcard flew through the air and literally wedged itself underneath my shoe. I felt compelled to pick it up. It was a white card, and in large black letters it said, "Abortion – Don't Do It." I was very taken aback and took it as a sign that I had made the right decision in continuing with the pregnancy.

I went home, and for the rest of my pregnancy, I decided to visualize my baby growing healthily. I imagined a piece of metal covering my baby's brain, ensuring that the fluid-filled sac wouldn't put any pressure on it and, therefore, protecting it from being damaged. I imagined giving birth to a healthy baby, and I looked forward to every doctor's appointment, because I knew that each time I would be told my baby was healthy. I visualized my baby playing with her big sister, and I gave thanks every day for being blessed with a healthy child.

I continued to have very regular checkups throughout my pregnancy, and at every appointment I was assured – much to the doctor's amazement – that there was nothing wrong with my baby. At my very last appointment at *thirty-seven weeks*, I was told that the fluid-filled sac on our baby's head had not grown and had not put any pressure on her brain. I was told that I would give birth to a perfectly healthy baby. The doctor also mentioned that he had not often seen this condition end in a positive way.

Our beautiful daughter, Scarlett Emmie, was born on Wednesday, October 2, 2013, and is absolutely perfect! She is *beautiful* and *healthy*! All the doctors involved have been to see her, and they are amazed that her brain was not affected.

After that first doctor's appointment, I was told that there would definitely be something wrong with my baby; they just didn't know how severe it would be. It turned out that they were wrong. I have no doubt that my positivity not only gave me the strength to carry on, it also gave my baby the strength to grow healthily without any complications.

At five months old, Scarlett had a minor operation to remove the fluid-filled sac, and she continues to develop just as she should.

I have The Secret to thank for her health and my strength. I look at her and can't believe how perfect she is! Miracles can happen!

~ *Emily*, London, England

Faith was also absolutely essential to the survival of Franci's son, Kyle, who was born prematurely with a hole in his heart.

KYLE'S HEART

My son, Kyle, was born nine weeks early. He was so tiny but so strong. When I was in the operating room, they warned me that he wouldn't cry because his lungs were not developed. But when I heard a sound a few minutes later and asked, "What was that?" a nurse replied, "Your son." My husband told me later that he had heard it outside the operating room.

It was a long road to wellness for Kyle. Each day I was amazed by his strength and spirit. He left the hospital five weeks to the day after his birth without any monitors. The doctors called it amazing!

Unfortunately, however, he also had a hole in his heart that would need correcting by the time he was two. The doctors told us that a hole that size would not close on its own. My baby would need open-heart surgery.

My aunt told me to visualize his heart closing up and to say each day, "Kyle is heart-healthy! Kyle is heart-healthy!" I visualized and said my mantra over and over every day.

When we took Kyle for his pre-op appointment, the cardiologist ran the usual tests, the EKG, and the ultrasound of Kyle's heart, and the hole had closed by more than 50 percent. The procedure was put off for six months with the additional possibility of a less invasive alternative to open-heart surgery. I continued to visualize my child with a healthy heart, and six months later, the hole had closed even more.

Once more the doctor said, "Let's wait." We waited and watched Kyle thrive. My little boy, who used to get winded when walking across a room, was now running at top speed and not slowing down to catch his breath. I continued to visualize and believe.

At our final appointment, after all the usual tests, the cardiologist came bounding into the room and said, "I never want to see you here again. The hole is closed." He showed me the X-ray, and it was. The doctor called it a major miracle. He had never seen a hole that size close in such a short amount of time.

Because of the power of The Secret, my son has truly been given a new life.

~ *Franci K.,* Doylestown, Pennsylvania, USA

You may wonder how anyone can maintain unwavering faith in a positive outcome when they are in the midst of a health crisis. As these stories demonstrate, the intention and power of the human spirit is stronger than any adverse event or situation.

Healing a Pet

Whatever Secret practices we can use to heal ourselves or our children we can also use for our animals. While you cannot override anyone's experience if their journey is meant to take a different path, animals are very receptive to positive thoughts and feelings.

HUGE TUMOR – GONE!

When my beloved German shepherd was ten years old, the vet found a very large tumor, about the size of a grapefruit, on her liver. I had just been divorced and was moving, so I decided I could not go into panic mode. At the time I didn't know The Secret, so I didn't try to heal it, I just didn't give it any attention.

It took a few months to find a new home and settle in. Then I found a local vet and took my German shepherd for an examination. I didn't mention the tumor. I was hoping the previous vet was wrong. But the new doctor told me the same thing: a huge tumor was on her liver. The vet said we could do more tests to find out exactly what kind of cancer it was, but it seemed extremely likely to be "bad," and since my dog was already at the end of her normal life span, which is eight to ten years for German shepherds, that didn't make a lot of sense to me. I wasn't going to put her through any more procedures that were unlikely to help her.

Then I discovered The Secret, and I went straight to work. I told her every night that she was completely healed. I didn't

want to say that the tumor was gone, since I knew not to
mention the tumor at all. At first it was hard to think of how
to say things positively. So I thought about it and started
telling her that all her organs worked perfectly and her
digestive system worked perfectly. I told her she was in perfect
health. I knew in my heart that she was healed. I told her this
every night and whenever I thought of it during the day. I
didn't worry at all. I didn't have any negative thoughts. I was
completely confident that she was healed.

Well, I went back to the vet four months later. She checked
my dog and then checked her again and then again. The vet
couldn't believe it; the tumor was totally gone. She asked what
I had done, and I told her I had prayed. I thought that would
be a description that she could understand. The vet even
wrote "prayers" in the notes.

~ *Lucinda M.*, California, USA

Lucinda understood that if her affirmations were to work,
she had to talk to her dog *as if* she were perfectly healthy.
Focusing on the tumor would only be giving it more
power.

You can change the path of your life from dark to light or from negative to positive. Every single time you focus on the positive, you are bringing more light into your life, and you know that light removes all darkness. Gratitude, love, kind thoughts, words, and actions bring light and eliminate the darkness. Fill your life with the light of positivity.

— The Secret Daily Teachings

BELIEVING THE BEST

One day my wonderful twelve-year-old cocker spaniel went off his food, which was absolutely unheard of. He was also struggling to drink, and the water just seemed to pour out of his mouth instead of his being able to swallow.

I took him to the vet, and while we were in the waiting room, blood started to gush from his mouth. We were rushed into the examining room, and I was told that he would need to be anesthetized to investigate the problem; given his age, they said, it could be an abscess from a rotten tooth. I left him at the vet with arrangements to pick him up later.

Then came the shocking phone call.

The vet telephoned while my dog was on the operating table. They had found a massive tumor growing inside his tongue and another underneath his tongue. He also had a lump on his chest. The vet stated that it was a really aggressive form of cancer and the kindest thing would be not to wake him from the anesthetic but to let him drift off to sleep.

I was horrified and mortified. However, I could not let my dog be put to sleep without being certain of the diagnosis. Going against the vet's wishes, I instructed him to take biopsies of all the lumps and also to do any necessary dental work. He did as I asked, all the while making me feel as if I were letting my dog suffer unnecessarily and that the dental work would just increase my bill while the dog would not have the time to enjoy its benefits since he probably had no more than two weeks to live.

When I picked him up and brought him home, the whole family was devastated. That night he was in so much pain that I really did feel I had been selfish and, for a brief time, regretted my decision.

And then I remembered the teachings of The Secret.

From that point on, with every fiber of my body, I put all my energy into believing that he had an infection, no cancer, and that he would be fine. I thanked the Universe every spare moment, over and over again, for his healing and being back to his old self. I can truly say that I actually believed it was so and relayed to anyone who would listen that he was fine and well on the road to recovery!

We had a checkup at the vet a couple of days later, at which time I was given painkillers and antibiotics and told there was nothing more to be done than to make him comfortable. During the week that followed, I put my full trust into his being cured and refused to let myself even think of any other outcome.

Finally, the vet called with the biopsy results. He was completely shocked, but all tests had come back negative for cancer.

I was told that it was highly likely they had simply missed the cancer cells, but it was a bit of a fluke that all three biopsies were negative. For me, it wasn't a fluke or an incorrect result. To top it all off, none of his teeth was bad or needed to be removed!

I thank the Universe every day for his health and the fact that I didn't listen to the vet on that miserable day when everything looked bleak!

~ *Jane J.*, Ascot, Berkshire, England

Happiness Is a Health Elixir

If you make a decision that from here onward you will give the majority of your attention to happy thoughts, you will begin a process of purifying your body. Those happy thoughts will supply your body with the greatest health-booster you could possibly give it.

There are endless excuses not to be happy. But if you put happiness off by saying "I'll be happy when . . ." you'll not only be delaying happiness for the rest of your life, you'll also be diminishing the health of your body. Happiness is your body's miracle health elixir, so be happy now, no excuses!

To be equally balanced between your heart and your mind is to live a life of bliss. When your heart and mind are balanced, your body is in complete harmony. And so is your life.

– The Secret Daily Teachings

Keys To Health

☞ *At some point every so-called incurable disease has been cured. There are no hopeless cases.*

☞ *Healing through the mind can work harmoniously with traditional medicine.*

☞ *If you can imagine and feel being well, you can receive it.*

☞ *If you have negative beliefs about your health, you need to change your mind to see your health change.*

☞ *Think thoughts of well-being. Speak words of well-being. And imagine yourself completely well.*

☞ *No matter what might have manifested, you can change it – with one positive thought and then another.*

☞ *To keep your body and mind healthy, don't believe negative thoughts. Instead, turn your mind to positive thoughts of beauty, love, gratitude, and joy.*

☞ *Visualize and let positive pictures of health flood your mind and body.*

☞ *Happiness is your body's miracle health elixir. Give your attention to happy thoughts, and begin the process of purifying your body.*

☞ *You can use your positive thoughts and feelings to help heal a child or a pet as you would yourself.*

If there was a particular . . . job you wanted, and you didn't get it, the Universe is telling you that it was not good enough and did not match your dream. It is also telling you that it has something BETTER and more worthy of you.

Something better is coming . . . you're allowed to be excited!

– The Secret Daily Teachings

How I Used The Secret for My Career

Because all of The Secret principles and practices can be used to attract whatever you want to bring into your life, there is no "dead-end job" you can't turn around or escape; there is no "glass ceiling" you can't shatter; there is no "dream job" you can't have.

Focus on the Positive; Ignore Anything Negative

If the circumstances of your life aren't going the way you hoped they would, it's easy to get down and depressed. But as you now know, and so many people around the world have learned, negative thoughts always attract negative circumstances. On the other hand, when you focus your thoughts on something you want, and you hold that focus, you are in that moment summoning what you want with the mightiest power in the Universe.

HARASSED IN EVERY JOB

For years I was getting angrier and angrier in jobs. I always seemed to find the worst possible employer to work for. It was all God's fault, and the angrier I got at God, the worse things seemed to get and the more I hated God.

When I started working for a local printer doing electronic pre-press, I was always looking around to see if this was going to be the same-old-same-old, or if *this* place might be different. As far as I could see, everyone was great to work with. I was actually having a good time and enjoying my coworkers and supervisor – until, three months after I started, the printer decided to branch out into digital printing and asked if I would do the electronic pre-press for the new digital printer. I said, "Sure, I'd love to."

They made the one guy who couldn't get along with anyone my supervisor. He harassed me, left mean notes on my chair when I went to lunch, and was making an enormous number of errors that he blamed on me.

Long story short, they fired me after six months.

I felt suicidal. I thought it was over. I was sick of this. I saw God up there laughing at me. I hated like I'd never hated in my life.

A friend gave me *The Secret* DVD, and I saw for the first time how I had created that whole reality of being harassed in every job I had. It all made so much sense. My thoughts had been: *He better not talk to me like that again; Why is it I always end up next to the most difficult person in the company to work with?; I'm not good enough, I hope I don't get fired; I hope they don't figure out that I don't know what I'm doing; I hope they don't figure out I'm a fake* . . . Those are just *some* of the many negative thoughts that were constantly going through my mind.

I wrote down all those thoughts, I looked at them in all their problematic ugliness, and I wrote their opposite positive thoughts on the other side of the page. At first it felt worse, so I rephrased the positive thoughts as questions and desires: "What would it feel like to know I can work with easygoing, moral people? What would it feel like to make more money than I've ever made before? I'd love to work for a publisher one day; that would be cool; I want to be working by [and filled in the date]."

On the very date I'd filled in, I got called for an interview with a publisher and got the job. Although I am no longer at that job, my coworkers were among the most easygoing, understanding, and *moral* people I'd ever met. I'd had no idea companies like that really existed.

And yes, I was making more money than I'd ever made in the past.

Do I still get fearful thoughts? Yes. Do I entertain them? Not for long. I know I don't have to. Before, I didn't know I had a choice. Now, when a negative thought comes up, I focus on its opposite, or if that's too extreme for me to comprehend at the moment, I change it to a question: "What would it feel like if . . . ?" And that has been a very powerful tool for me.

I'm definitely not perfect at this. I take a few steps backward some days, more often than I like to admit. But I'm now running my own small business and making even more money than I have in the past. My business is growing rapidly, and I'm at a point where I need to start thinking of expanding to the next level.

I hope everyone out there gives this a shot. It really works. And if it doesn't work for you, ask, "What would it feel like if it DID work for me?" And it will work.

~ *Annette,* Florida, USA

You cannot ever say the law of attraction is not working, because it is working all the time. If you don't have what you want, you are seeing the effect of your use of the law. If you don't have what you want, then you are creating not having what you want. You are still creating and the law is still responding to you.

If you understand this, then you can redirect your incredible power to attract what you want.

– The Secret Daily Teachings

WHAT GETS YOU TO BELIEVE?

After I graduated from college, I struggled for many months to get a job. I read *The Secret* many times and watched the movie, and while it totally changed my way of thinking and gave me a better outlook on life, I was still having trouble getting myself to believe that I already had a job, which was what I wanted most from the Universe.

One day, after a week of applying for countless jobs without getting a response, I had an epiphany. I was trying to remain very optimistic and writing in my journal every day that I was grateful for the job I had, but I truly wasn't acting or thinking as if I already had a job. I realized that sitting at home, just applying for jobs, and hoping that one would come my way wasn't getting me anywhere, because I was telling myself through my thoughts and actions that I would always be looking for a job! I figured out that I had to live as though I were already employed.

I began to get up extra early, as I would if I had to go to work in the morning, and instead of searching for jobs every day and writing in my journal about being grateful that a job was coming, I would write how grateful I was that each day at work was successful and that I loved where I was working and the people I worked with. I planned out outfits to wear for the workweek and set up a savings account for my paychecks. I hung out with friends who had jobs after they got home from work and listened to them talk about their jobs without having the feelings of jealousy or inadequacy I used to have, because I knew that I too had a job and, therefore, had no reason to feel any resentment. I also brushed up on my typing and computer skills.

Pretty soon I really did believe and feel as though I had a job and a schedule to adhere to.

About two weeks after I started "pretending" that I had a job, someone told me about a position that would be perfect for me. Even before I went for the interview, I knew I would get the job, and I did! The most amazing part is that things at my new job are going almost exactly as I had written about them in my journal. Now I write about how I want things to go every day, and it always works out.

I am so grateful to The Secret, because if I had never studied its teachings, I would never have known that things have to be believed before they can happen, and I would never be living as I do now.

~ *Kate,* Long Island, New York, USA

Initially, Kate's actions were not matched to her desires, so she was actually blocking herself from receiving what she wanted. Once she began *acting as if* she had a job, she actually started to *believe* it, and once she believed it, she received it.

WHEN THERE'S NOTHING LEFT, YOU HAVE THE SECRET!

After I was laid off from a well-paying job that I absolutely loved, it took me fifteen long, depressing, painstaking months to secure another full-time position, and even that was a dead-end entry-level job that paid half of what I'd been earning and for which I was highly overqualified. I hated it, but I stuck it out for four long years, thinking that "something good" would come of this. Oh, how WRONG was I.

"Be grateful and don't make waves, man" was my mantra. Although I hated every hour of my workday, I learned to bury my feelings and maintain a minute ray of hope that something else would open up within the company.

Finally, after applying for more than seventy-five positions, being called for about five interviews, and receiving no offers, I was done. One day I just decided that I MUST STOP allowing life to happen TO me and start making it happen FOR me!

Enter The Secret! I'd read *The Secret* about a year prior to my day of reckoning and finally decided to use it. I created a daily journal, and in the course of my workday, I would record a world in which I enjoyed my job. I used all of the tips from *The Secret* by absolutely immersing myself in the world I created. I lived that world daily with every one of my senses. I saw my office; I touched the keyboard of my computer; I smelled the lemon Pledge scent emanating from my huge mahogany desk; I engaged in audible conversations with my team (I even gave my team members first and last names, physical traits, and personalities); I tasted the carne asada tacos I ate during my lunch breaks. I attended meetings and gave presentations. I was there, man! I was really THERE!

Then the Universe began to make things happen. I received more interviews. Then second interviews! Then, finally, TWO offers of jobs I knew I wanted and would enjoy, and I accepted one of those jobs!

The Secret: Believe it! Feel it! See it! Touch it! Live it! Expect it!

~ *Kelly,* Indiana, USA

Kelly threw himself into manifesting a life that was the complete opposite of the one he was living. He used all of his senses to visualize every aspect of what he wanted until he truly believed that he was living it. He is proof positive that every single second is an opportunity to change your life.

If your day is not going well, stop and deliberately change your thoughts and feelings. If your day is going swimmingly, keep doing what you are doing.

– The Secret Daily Teachings

How *Is Not Your Job*

Just like anything else you want to bring into your life, *how* you will receive the job or career opportunity of your dreams is not something you should be concerned about. The Universe will move all people, circumstances, and events to manifest your desire in an orchestration that would be impossible for you to arrange. So forget about how you will receive what you've asked for and instead feel as if you already have it.

AT TWENTY-FIVE YEARS OLD, I GOT MY BOOK PUBLISHED!!!

After watching *The Secret,* I wrote all of my goals on a piece of paper and posted it above my desk. One of my seven major goals was to have my book of poems published by a major press. For two months after watching *The Secret,* I did nothing but visualize and evoke the feelings of ecstatic empowerment that come with having a book published.

Now, bear in mind that I didn't know how I would do this. I just knew that I would do it. Most established poets will tell you that you must have had at least the majority of the poems in your book published in well-known magazines before you have any hope of getting them published in book form.

I refused to believe that. I simply believed that my book would be published and on the shelves of Barnes & Noble within a year.

Two weeks after I started my visualization, I received an email from the editor of a well-known press saying that he was considering the manuscript I had submitted to him two months before and had totally forgotten about! I was floored.

So, I printed out the painting that I wanted for my book cover and wrote the title on the front. I wrote my list of acknowledgments, and I wrote his acceptance email to me and posted it above my bed. I continuously visualized what I would do when I received the good news: going to class and uncorking a bottle of champagne; calling my parents. I designed invitations to the celebration I would have when I received the good news. I told a few of my students that I had published a book.

Soon enough, I got a phone call from an unfamiliar area code. It was the editor of the press saying that he'd like to publish my book of poems and would send me a contract and further information ASAP. This stuff works!!!!

~ *Maria,* New York, USA

If you're like a cat on a hot tin roof, wanting to meddle in *how* your desire will come about, understand this: if you take even one step toward the Universe's job of *how*, you cancel your creation. Why? Because your actions are saying you don't have what you want, and you will then continue to attract not having what you want.

Maria didn't know *how* her dream of becoming a published poet would come about, but she was wise enough to take very specific actions as if it had already happened. Those are the kinds of actions that speed up manifestation!

HOPE

I was a student of self-help books for many years. I had tried and tried for years to do everything I had learned, but just could not get it to click. Then, a few years ago, I discovered *The Secret*, and it put together, all in one place, everything I had learned over the years and made that very easy to understand and apply. It was the missing link for me. Ask, Believe, and Receive. *That* did it! That was the essence, and the teachings made it so simple. Fantastic.

When I discovered *The Secret*, I was in a horrible marriage and a dead-end job. Everything I tried seemed to fail, and I did not understand why, because I had always thought of myself as a positive guy and a self-help guru.

I started applying The Secret to all aspects of my life and immediately started seeing changes for the better.

The first thing to change was my career. I had been a professional actor in my twenties, but when I had children at thirty, I got a "real job." I was miserable but thought it had to be that way. After reading *The Secret,* I resigned from my good-paying "stable" job. No real plans or strategy, just faith and putting in an order to the Universe for a career in my passion and love for acting.

Within three months, I had a small role in a low-budget film. Two more roles came in the six months after that. I began placing bigger orders. I wanted to live a stress-free lifestyle, big money, to have my mortgage and living expenses taken care of.

Then I went on an audition that changed my life. It was for a one-year acting job in Singapore! I didn't question the Universe, I just said thank you, held on, and have been on a whirlwind ride ever since.

I am no longer in a horrible marriage, and my relationship with my ex is better than it ever has been. My kids and I have a very close relationship, and they have been able to see parts of the world I never imagined being able to show them. I get to play for a living, doing what I love. All of my living expenses are taken care of for me. I live in a beautiful high-rise condo and don't pay a cent. My salary is more than I have ever made in my life, and I work fewer hours than I have ever worked before. The work doesn't feel like work, and I get to travel all over the place.

I feel years younger, I am way happier, and I have very little stress. Ever!!

I was one of those people who did not truly believe I could have all of this. That was for the "other" guy. I am a true believer now.

I want to thank Rhonda and thank the Universe for all of the blessings in this life, not just the material but the intangible, emotional, and spiritual blessings.

~ *Darrell B.*, Singapore

Darrell received everything he wanted even though he'd had no idea *how* that would happen, and the same is true for Roland, whose story follows. The other thing they had in common was a really clear idea of what they wanted and an unwavering belief that they would receive it.

WHERE THERE'S A WILL, THERE'S A WAY!

I would like to start by expressing my sincere gratitude to The Secret Team for bringing The Secret to the world and making it accessible to those of us who otherwise may never have discovered it.

Starting from the age of twelve, I've always wanted to live in Los Angeles and be a professional working drummer. Less than 1 percent of musicians actually make a living playing music. I'd realized some moderate success where I lived but had never been in a position to do only that without some kind of day job. I always felt like I belonged in a place like L.A., where the music and the industry flourish, and the sun shines 95 percent of the time.

On some level, I guess I have employed some rules of The Secret without realizing it, as I never seem to worry about money, and it always seems to be there when I need it. However, since watching *The Secret,* I have become more powerful than ever. I bought the audiobook and began listening to it every day, and still do as much as possible. I've been concentrating on learning every aspect of it and employing every bit.

I quit my job three months ago and just felt in my heart it was the right thing to do. I had no idea what I would do for money or where I was going from there. Still, I felt extremely relaxed and had faith that everything would be fine and work itself out. As a result, a temporary job materialized, and I made more than $10,000 in two months, which is more than I had been making. When that ended, I had no idea what to do next or where my next paycheck was coming from. Then I got a call from a cruise line operating out of L.A., saying that they wanted to use our band to develop a new series of shows for their ships. We would be working out of L.A. in their big production studio.

All I had been doing was keeping in good spirits, imagining myself living in L.A., working as a musician, and being prosperous and successful. Everything is falling into place, one thing at a time, in ways I couldn't have imagined. It's absolutely amazing how it is working, and it truly feels like it's only the very beginning.

Just listening to the audiobook makes me so happy and puts me in such a great mood, my eyes literally start to tear. I can't explain it. Even if all I got out of this was a way to look at life and think more positively, that alone would be an amazing gift. This, however, is so much more; thank you for that.

~ *Roland C.,* Nanaimo, Canada

By learning about The Secret, Roland became aware that he had the power within him to attract the career he wanted. We can all have, be, or do anything; there are no limits. We just need to figure out what we *really* want and ask for it.

Sometimes we may have good reason to wonder *how* we're going to get what we want. That was certainly true for the person in the next story. Despite the fact that every requirement for a particular dance audition suggested it would be impossible for her to get the job, she decided to test The Secret for herself!

BOLD AUDITION

I must admit that after reading *The Secret*, I was a bit dubious, but thought I would try it out with small things such as wanting someone to call me or not missing my train. Then, still not totally convinced that these weren't just coincidence, I thought I would try for something bigger.

My agent phoned to tell me about a casting call for a female dancer to be in a commercial. She wanted to send me for the job, but – and this was a big BUT – they wanted a white blonde. I'm black, so I was wondering why she had bothered, but I said I would go anyway.

Not really thinking about it much (you tend not to because it's so disappointing when you don't get a job), I went to the audition. Everyone there was white, and while I was sitting there, I realized I really, really wanted the job. So here was the perfect opportunity to see if The Secret worked! I started to imagine getting it and seeing my face on TV, people calling me to congratulate me, and this job leading to other jobs.

When it was my turn to see the casting director, I felt totally confident. I danced my little heart out and left!

I was thinking about the job all the way home, and when I arrived, I wrote the name of the product on a Post-it and stuck it on my wardrobe. I kept envisioning getting the job and how I would react when I was told the news.

The next day while I was on a different job, I got a call from my agent. "I have some good news – " She didn't even have to complete the sentence. I knew why she was calling. I GOT THE JOB!!!! I was ecstatic. Even though I'd told myself the job was mine, it was still so amazing when I was told.

Now I know that I can be more ambitious and really be in control of my future. That's so exciting.

~ *K.,* London, England

Create Your Dream Salary

In our next story, Yana had a particular job in mind, as well as a particular salary, and she used the power of affirmation to attract exactly what she desired.

THE JOB

After losing a very well-paying job, I moved from one temp job to another, to total unemployment, and finally, to a permanent part-time position paying $10 an hour. Then, just two days after I started, I was told that my hours were being cut in half, from twenty hours a week to ten. There was no way I could live on $100 a week.

I walked home from work that day feeling sad and discouraged. When I got into my apartment, I felt an overwhelming urge to watch *The Secret,* even though I didn't have much more energy than it would take to sit and worry about what I was going to do without a regular job and more money. After I watched the movie, I got out my journal and wrote this affirmation:

"Within the coming days, I am manifesting a great administrative position within walking distance of my home. "At this job I make at least $30,000 per year. The people I work with are joyful, kind-hearted, and cooperative. The work I perform I find interesting, and I am greatly appreciated by my coworkers and supervisors. I am paid weekly, arrive on time or early every Monday through Friday, and I thoroughly enjoy every day that I go to this job. I am thankful for the inclusive and clear process that has manifested my perfect new job right now."

I said the affirmation throughout the next day, and I could *feel* joy when I said it. A feeling of excitement washed over me every time I thought about this new job. I was so excited!

While I was at work that day, my cell phone kept ringing. I missed three back-to-back calls, all from the same number, and all within minutes of one another. During a break, I checked my messages, and the call turned out to be from a temp agency I had registered with a couple of years before.

When I returned the call, the receptionist said that they had been trying to reach me because they had a job for me and it would be starting the next day. The job was paying exactly what I was asking for in my affirmation, and when I asked her where it was, she said it was at a design firm that was a five-minute walk from my house. And to cap it all off, it was a permanent position.

I started my job two days after writing my affirmation, and it is just as wonderful today as it was the first day I arrived.

~ *Yana F.*, Baltimore, Maryland, USA

Yana's affirmation included being grateful for her new job and her new salary *as if* she had received them. Gratitude is a bridge that will take you from poverty to riches. The more grateful you can be for the money you have, even if you don't have very much, the more riches you will receive. And the more you complain about money, the poorer you will become.

DOUBLE OR NOTHING!

When I started my journalism career, my family offered me tons of support, which gave me the necessary drive to pursue my goal. I got a job at a local magazine company that paid little but showed a lot of promise. I made just enough to cover my rent, and my parents gave me just enough to make it through the month.

As the months went by, however, my dad started getting tired of paying most of my bills and went out of his way to show it. I understood that he wanted me to be more independent, but I started to become desperate. I wanted to make my folks happy, and I wanted to make enough money to be my own man. My desperation turned into depression as the end of the year approached, and I gave up hoping for the raise I'd been promised. I started to expect only bad things, and guess what? That's exactly what I got.

My depression got to a point where I started feeling sick and tired all the time. Things were looking bad, and I just started hoping for a way out of all this. Then, out of the blue, a friend of mine who was aware of my situation asked me if I knew about *The Secret*. She gave me a copy of the DVD and asked me to just give it a chance. I'm not much into self-help advice, but I watched it that very night. What everyone on the DVD said was about me; I was causing bad things to happen to me through my thoughts. I cried that night, not sad tears but tears of joy. I knew I was going to be all right.

I began to use The Secret that very night. I began to think good thoughts, thoughts of wealth and happiness. I began to thank the Universe for the things I never thought about in my life, like my good health, the love of friends, even my job.

At the end of December, the company manager called me into his office and told me I would be getting a raise. The raise was small, and it wouldn't cover all my expenses, but I thanked him and the Universe because I knew that I had asked, believed, and the receiving had begun.

At the beginning of January, I asked the Universe for something I now know is very possible. I asked for my monthly salary to double. I had no idea how it would happen, but I just believed it would. The Universe got to work immediately. I couldn't see it happening, but I knew in my heart that it was.

Four months later, in April, I was asked to move to a different magazine within the same company. And guess what? The pay was twice my salary at the time. I knew it was because I believed. Then I thought, *Hey, if it worked once, it could work again.* I asked the Universe again for double my new salary. You won't believe it, but four months later, the manager of the digital department asked me to join his team. And the pay? You guessed it: double my current salary.

The Secret has turned my life totally around. It's hard to believe that one year was just as bad as I wanted it to be, and the next year was as good as I visualized and believed it to be. Every day is a gift these days. I know now that I am special and unique. The Universe is my friend and responds to my thoughts; my story is proof that The Secret truly works.

So, you're probably wondering if I asked the Universe to double my salary yet again. Nope. I asked for happiness and abundance, and that's what I'm receiving every day.

~ *Alan,* Nairobi, Kenya

Alan thanked the Universe for what he already had as well as what he wanted to receive, and then he let the law of attraction do its work without worrying about how it would happen or trying to help it along.

THE WINNING COMBINATION

Several years ago, the employees at the small chiropractic office where I worked saw that the business numbers were decreasing. No one had received a raise in more than three years. Something had to change. We loved our jobs, but the cost of living was going up, and we were all starting to look for new jobs or second jobs.

The staff met on a day without the doctors being present and talked about wanting a raise. We knew that in order for that to happen, we had to set goals for our office and fill the schedules for all the doctors. We started with weekly and monthly goals. Once these goals were in place, we figured that a 25 percent raise would make up for the lack of raises over the last few years. But most of all, we needed to determine how soon we wanted our raise. We decided on October 15, an unusual time of the year for giving raises.

We set our plan in motion. We created a saying: "Life is good at 25 percent!" and posted it on each of our desks. Every day we would focus on the schedule being full for all the doctors. If it was not full enough, we would say, "We need ten more established patients and two new patients," and sure enough, the phone would start ringing! Soon the doctors were so busy that they complained about how tired they were at the end of the day.

At the beginning of October, the staff met once more to review our goals and our gratitude lists. We thought that the next office meeting would be a great time to do a presentation of our goals and how they came about. On the day of the meeting, we were ready, but the doctors had a lot on the agenda and we didn't get to do our presentation. We were disappointed, and October 15 was just two days away, but we kept on focusing and saying, "Life is good at 25 percent!"

Well, the fifteenth came and went. Our next pay period was coming up, and the doctors had met with our accountant. A few days later, our boss asked me to meet with her. I had no idea why, but her opening line was that we had been doing a great job and we were all getting a raise, which would be retroactive to October 15. All but one of us got 25 percent, and she got 20 percent. My eyes filled up with tears as I told the doctor that we had used The Secret to reach the goals we had set for the office and our 25 percent raise.

We saved our jobs, made some money, and boosted the morale in the office. The staff is now meeting and improving our personal lives using The Secret, and we encourage our patients to borrow the DVD from our office anytime they want.

~ *Loretta,* Washington, USA

There is no doubt that when two or more people focus on attracting the same desire, they create a very powerful force. Each person adds their energy and belief, which makes for a winning combination.

Let Loretta's story inspire you. If you work with a team of people, together you can focus on a mutual desire that will benefit everyone. Just imagine what you can achieve together!

Ultimately, you have the power to create whatever you want by yourself, but when we join forces with others, it can help us to increase our belief factor so much that manifestation happens really quickly.

Do What You Love

For the people whose stories I'm about to share, being able to do what they loved was their greatest wish. For some the money was also important, but others simply believed that if they followed their dream, the Universe would deliver the money they needed. A perfect example of this is the story of Dallas, below.

TWO WEEKS TO A NEW LIFE

I almost gave up on the law of attraction when, after living the life of my dreams, I found myself living on the street for two years. I felt abandoned by everyone. It was the middle of winter and I had nowhere to go, so I traveled the country looking for employment, but with no luck.

I'd heard it was possible to change your life in thirty days using the law of attraction, so I put it to the ultimate test. The knowledge from *The Secret* became part of my daily reading/ listening, and I put into place everything I heard. Little did I know how fast things would come to me.

I *needed* a job, any job, but I *wanted* a job that provided me freedom, put me in the center of a lot of action, allowed me to contribute to and expand the company while being appreciated for my work. I was so happy *knowing* that it was on the way. As long as I felt that way, it *had* to.

Within two weeks, as the result of a chance meeting, I landed a job as a radio DJ. After seven months, I'd increased advertising revenue by 2,000 percent and created a new division specifically to help artists raise money (without relying on CD sales or getting gigs). I manage up-and-coming artists, have formed an artist collaborative to assist new talent in making it in the industry, and am currently working on a clothing line with a business partner. My boss loves my work, and I've been called our station's best DJ, which was exactly my intention.

I now have my dream job, and I'm so happy and grateful for the position I'm in. Great things just keep coming my way, and I'm always reaching for bigger and better dreams.

If anyone doubts The Secret, take it from me . . . *it works.*

~ *Dallas C.,* Winnipeg, Manitoba, Canada

Even though Dallas knew he needed money, his primary desire was to do something he loved. The result? He got both!

Even when you're sensing that the Universe is ready to deliver what you want most, you may have moments when doubts creep in. This may be especially true if you are thinking about the possible consequences of leaving a secure job in order to follow your dream.

If you ever find yourself in doubt, you can ask the Universe for evidence that you're making the right decision. Remember, you can ask for anything!

In the next story, Helen suffered serious doubts just before she was about to leave her job. And then the Universe stepped in and moved a few technical things to help her along with her decision.

EMAILS FROM THE UNIVERSE

I was first introduced to *The Secret* by a colleague several years ago, but, unfortunately, I was in such a negative place back then that, after reading a couple of pages, I was actually fearful of what reading the book would do to my life. How ridiculous that sounds now! Thankfully, it was recommended to me again by a friend, and this time I was more than ready to learn.

I cannot tell you how happy and excited I felt as I read each chapter. I was almost giddy, and after just the first day of reading it, I made a huge, life-changing decision.

I'd been considering leaving my part-time job as a designer to become a full-time freelance illustrator. I'd wanted to do that for as long as I can remember, but I had financial commitments and was reluctant to lose the regular, steady income. I kept telling myself I would just have to wait until I had enough money saved up. I was just too scared, despite my instincts screaming that it was the right thing to do.

Previously, I had been really unlucky in my career, with awful employers, stressful working environments, and multiple redundancies. Deep down I felt that I was being pushed to go it alone, but I was too afraid of letting myself and my family down.

After reading *The Secret*, I knew I had to do it, and strangely, I didn't have a shred of doubt; I knew I would be a success!

But when I was about to hand in my notice at work, the old doubting me returned. On the train traveling to work, I had butterflies in my stomach and kept asking myself if I was doing the right thing. Maybe I was being rash, selfish, what about money, etc. That was when the Universe stepped in to give me a huge nudge – just as I was about to chicken out!

While all these fearful thoughts were racing around my head, I glanced down at my iPhone, and it said I had thirty-seven new emails. I thought that was very odd, as it was really early in the morning and there had been none when I had checked it a few minutes before. But when I looked at all the "new" emails, they were actually all emails from . . . me! Ones I had sent to various people over the past *five years*, all in my inbox at the same time, and all of them had the same theme. Every single one of those emails was related to wanting to leave my job and work for myself! The first one I read was one I had sent to a recruitment agency when I had been made redundant for the third time. And the first sentence that jumped out at me was "I think somebody up there is trying to tell me something"! As soon as I read that, I got a shiver down my spine (I've got one now writing this). I was speechless. There were a few more to recruitment agencies (reminding me of how many times I'd been made redundant); there were ones I'd sent complaining about how much I disliked working for various bosses; there were ones relating to previous freelance children's book projects I had worked on and loved; but the oldest email was one I had sent several years before to my current agent saying how much I wanted to work as a freelance illustrator and asking if they would consider representing me. I didn't have that email saved anywhere on my computer, let alone my phone. I didn't even remember sending it, but there it was as a "new" email, along with all the others appearing in my inbox at the same time.

I knew then that somebody was trying to tell me I was doing the right thing and everything was going to be okay. I couldn't stop smiling all day and handed in my notice without a second thought.

Two months later, I couldn't believe how busy I was! To think I had doubted having enough money to pay the bills! When I wrote my desired first-year earnings on the blank check from The Secret website, it seemed ridiculously out of reach, but when I added up what I'd earned since the beginning of the year, I was actually on track to earn exactly that amount! I was already booked up with work for months in advance and had no doubts whatsoever that my success would continue.

Four years later, I'm still self-employed, and I've also had my dream come true this year: the first children's picture book I both wrote and illustrated is published and available worldwide.

I felt so privileged that day to receive such a huge message from the Universe, and am now thankful for all that is good in my life and enjoy visualizing my fabulous future!

~ *Helen,* Liverpool, England

If you're finding that doubts are really undermining your belief, increase your belief through visualization and affirmations. Alternatively, you can do something that makes you feel happy, because when you feel happy, doubts will disappear! Doubt is a negative state, and it cannot exist in the presence of the positive state of happiness.

HOW I GOT THE JOB OF MY DREAMS

When I was first introduced to The Secret, I didn't believe that it would really work, so I started reading the book just to prove it wrong.

At that time, I had been trying to get my dream job for almost four years. While I was reading the book, I decided to play a game. So I made a pay slip that included the salary I wanted, the country I wanted to work in, and the position I wanted to be in, and I posted it on my mirror. Every morning I would look at it and visualize myself at my desk in my new job. Then, as the day went on, I would list the things I was thankful for and I would say, "Thank you for everything I do and everything that happens to me."

Within five days, I received the job offer I'd been dreaming of in my email.

Thank you for sharing The Secret.

~ *Mireille D.*, Lebanon

Once you're familiar with The Secret, you come to understand that there are many practices through which you can reinforce your belief and, therefore, speed up the law of attraction. Acting *as if* you've already received what you want is one of the most powerful practices.

PLAYING THE PART

Some time ago I dropped everything. I quit my job as a pastry cook. I dropped out of culinary school. I broke up with my boyfriend of two years. I gave up all hope of a good life and believed myself to be worthless. After a month of suffering from a serious case of depression, I woke up one day and thought about *The Secret*. I'm not sure why it came to me, but I decided to look it up online and find out what it was all about. I watched the movie on the website and was so moved by it that I went to iTunes and bought the audiobook.

Up to that point I had been searching for jobs and not getting any responses. But I decided to use The Secret to summon a job to me. I really wanted to work in a veterinary hospital, so I sent my résumé to one close by my home. That's how it all began.

A few days later, I was lying around my apartment when the phone rang. I told myself, *That is someone calling to offer me a job.* The person on the phone was a manager at the animal hospital I'd applied to, offering me an interview. During the interview, I was extremely nervous, and it showed. Even though it wasn't my best interview, I went home and wrote, "I work at _____ Animal Hospital. It's located at _____, Chicago, IL. The phone number is _____." I did this several times until I actually believed it.

A day later, the manager called me again and was extremely enthusiastic, offering me a second, working interview. I gladly accepted. I felt that I already had the job, but now I had to decide how much money I wanted to make. In the days leading up to the second interview, I wrote out an entire budget focusing on a certain amount of income. I looked at it a few times a day, pretending that it was already in place in my life.

During the working interview, I pretended that I already had the position and that my coworkers were just showing me around my new office. At the end of the day, the manager told me he would call me the following Monday, after he had made a decision. Well, he did call me. He offered me the position and also the exact amount of money I had asked for in my budget. It was an amazing feeling.

At the moment I'm just practicing the art of gratitude and enjoying my life every single moment of the day. So far, I have asked for and received everything I need at the moment, but I know that if I should ever need anything else, I can always let the Universe know.

~ *Lindsey*, Chicago, Illinois, USA

It is easy to visualize having a specific job – seeing yourself arriving at work and walking through the door. It's easy to visualize opening your paycheck and seeing a particular figure. It's easy to visualize yourself being given the news of that promotion. When you visualize you have it now, you *feel* as though you have it now, and that's the cue for manifestation!

The law of attraction responds exactly to your thoughts and words, and so if you see something as being in the future you are actually stopping it from happening now.

You must feel it as though you have it now.

– The Secret Daily Teachings

Keys To Creating Your Career

- *You have the power within you to attract the job of your dreams if you figure out what you really want and ask for it.*

- *There is no dream job or salary you can't have if you believe in it and expect it.*

- *Focus your thoughts on what you want in your job or career, and hold that focus.*

- *Use all of your senses to visualize every aspect of the job or career you want until you really feel you are living it.*

- *Visualize your paycheck and see the particular figure that you want.*

- *How you will receive the job or career opportunity is not your concern.*

- *To dispel doubt, do something that makes you feel happy, or increase your belief through visualization and affirmations.*

☞ *To speed up manifestation, act as if you've already received the job of your dreams.*

☞ *When you love what you do, the money will follow.*

☞ *You can be or do anything – there are no limits.*

*As you give the best of you, you
will be staggered by the speed
that it comes back to you.*

– The Secret Daily Teachings

How I Used The Secret to Change My Life

There is a truth deep down inside of you that is waiting to be discovered, and that truth is this: *you deserve all the good things that life has to offer.* You know that inherently, because you feel awful when you are experiencing the lack of good things. All good things are your birthright! You are the creator of your life, and the law of attraction is your magnificent tool to create whatever you want.

Like Jenny in the next story, many of the people who have shared their stories thank me for changing their lives. In truth, they have brought about those changes by changing themselves. I am just enormously grateful to have been able to share The Secret with all of them.

THE LOWEST POINT IN THE VALLEY

"Things have to change or I don't think I can make it any longer" is how I felt the day before my thirtieth birthday. Although I was highly educated, I couldn't find permanent full-time work. I was single and didn't want to be; I was living with my parents; and I was generally miserable. I didn't need much to make me feel happy and fulfilled, but it seemed like what I did need was never going to happen for me.

The Secret truly saved my life. You see, when I hit rock bottom, I finally felt up to diving in and reading the book as a sort of "last resort." Silly me, *The Secret* should have been my *first* step, not the last one! The change for me was immediate, because the book was a true inspiration, and I thought, *Even if this "secret" does nothing else, at least it has lifted my spirits and given me hope.*

But it did much more than inspire . . . it changed my entire life! To make it even more amazing, it changed my life *exactly* as I envisioned it!

Two months after starting the practice of The Secret, I got an interview with an awesome company and ultimately landed the job of my dreams. Through the process of interviewing for that job, I met an amazing man who is everything I ever wanted in a partner. I'll finally be moving out on my own and starting the life that I had been hoping and wishing for. I wasted so much time feeling sorry for myself instead of realizing the power that I held within to get the things that I want.

I'm so appreciative that I was given this magnificent gift of The Secret, because I don't know what might have become of me without it.

~ *Jenny L.*, Detroit, Michigan, USA

Within you are the exact answers that you need to every single question, and so it is important that you discover answers for yourself. You must trust in yourself and all that you are.

– The Secret Daily Teachings

No Matter Where You Are Now, It Can All Change

The writers of the stories in the following pages describe themselves as having been damaged, destructive, drug-addicted, homeless, miserable, and a pretty big mess, to name just a few of the ways they've described themselves. What they all came to appreciate after learning about The Secret was that they could change their own lives by changing their thoughts – in other words, by changing themselves.

TURNING CHICKEN POOP INTO CHICKEN SOUP

When I look back on my past life, I can hardly believe I am now the same person. I am so happy and at peace! It was not always this way. I was blind to my good for more than thirty years.

As a little girl, I was raped hundreds of times by my father. I developed epilepsy (I think as a way to escape). I became a social outcast. My mother was in and out of mental hospitals her whole life, and my home for a while was an old station wagon we parked at the city dump. My food was supplied by the nearby KFC Dumpster. As a young adult, I quit high school and became addicted to drugs and all sorts of destructive behavior.

My life looked bleak, and I was convinced it was just my lot in life to suffer hard and play the part of damaged loser.

I managed to get a college degree but subsequently found that I could not hold a job more than three months. After being fired from my thirty-fourth (or so) job, I lost it and became more depressed than ever; I was trying so hard to better my life! I was on Prozac, Wellbutrin, and a host of other drugs the doctors thought would normalize me. Didn't work. Every day I prayed God would let me die.

I then married a man I didn't love because I thought I'd be homeless if I didn't. I kicked the drug habit but spent my days sleeping and watching TV – anything to block out reality.

My transformation began with my first visit (at my older half sister's urging) to the Church of Religious Science, whose teachings are a lot like those contained in *The Secret*. They told me profound things that got me thinking in the right direction, things very new to me, like "Just because you exist, you are great."

But it wasn't until watching *The Secret* that I experienced truly profound transformation. One area (of many) I had always been blocked in was making enough money to survive on my own. One night, after watching *The Secret* for perhaps the twenty-third time, I got up, went to my computer, and requested that the Universe guide me in finding a fun, easy, high-paying job. I typed the words *forensic* and *videography* into my search engine (because I enjoy anything related to both). What should pop up but the actual field of legal videography. I was so excited! I just knew that was the career for me without even knowing what was involved.

I took the steps required to become a certified legal videographer and started earning $75 per hour minimum (after a lifetime of earning minimum wage or less)!

I recently switched from legal videography to in-home-care providing. It turned out that in order to do some of the more in-depth legal videography, I needed a notary license, and I did not qualify to get one. So I turned to my other passion, helping elderly people live better lives, which is what I would have done in the first place had I known that people got paid, let alone paid well, for doing this sort of work.

So I have started another business, providing in-home companion and health care for seniors or anyone else who may need it: disabled, post-operative folks, etc. I love what I do – it's amazingly rewarding! I tell everyone how lucky I feel to Love for a Living!

Other areas of my life are transformed too: I no longer take pills to get happy; I experience joy every day on my own! I quit smoking cigarettes. I work out five days a week and love it. I divorced the man whom I used to wholly depend upon. I can now say I love myself the way I am (this is *huge*, since when I was younger, I used to burn myself and actually punch myself with all my strength while screaming "I hate *you*" to the mirror because my self-loathing ran so deep).

I have a wonderful circle of positive-minded friends. I love life; I love Mondays; I have made peace with my dad. I find ecstatic joy in the simplest things; a cooling breeze on my neck can bring me to tears of happiness! It is really hard to put into words how wonderful my life is now. I feel solidly healthy, happy, prosperous, confident, energetic, accepting, trusting, and perhaps, more than anything, *grateful* for *everything* and *everyone* in my life! The Secret is just one more thing I am deeply grateful for. Thank you.

~ *K.*, California, USA

Because of experiences in childhood, we tend to think of ourselves as unworthy. If you do not treat yourself with love and respect, you are telling the Universe that you are not important enough, worthy enough, or deserving. You will experience more situations of people not treating you well –

such as being fired from thirty-four jobs. If you change how you feel by changing the way you think of yourself, you will also change the way you are treated by others.

> *The entire world and every single detail in your day are all showing you the frequency within you. The evidence of your frequency is speaking to you in every moment through the people whom you experience, the circumstances, and the events.*
>
> *Life is mirroring back to you what you are feeling inside you.*
>
> **– The Secret Daily Teachings**

MY ONLY CHANCE

I am twenty-nine years old and live in a lovely house in Melbourne, Australia, with my boyfriend, who is a police officer, and our beautiful identical-twin daughters, Melinda and Madeline.

Sounds great, doesn't it? Well, it is. However, life hasn't always been this happy. I came from a life of broken relationships and depression. My parents separated when I was four years old, and I didn't have a happy childhood. I got into relationships from a very young age, thinking they would make me happy, since I was searching for what I'd missed as a child. Instead of making me happy, they only led to misery and disappointment.

By the age of twenty-four, my life had plummeted to new lows, even to the extent of an attempted suicide. I had separated from my partner, I was broke, depressed, living with my mother, and I had no career.

One day I went into a new-age store, and the man who owned it gave me a copy of *The Secret* DVD. I took it home and watched it, and I agreed with the principles of it, but I just thought, *That's nice,* and filed it away with my other DVDs.

Life continued to be depressing, until one day I didn't feel like I could take any more of it. That was when I realized that using The Secret was my only chance ever to be happy. I began to really apply the principles. I made a definite decision as to what I really wanted in life, I created a vision board, and I began to live/feel/act as if those things were now a reality. Putting aside my doubts and fears about "how" all this would happen was difficult in the beginning, but I nevertheless persisted, giving thanks that the life I wanted was already a reality. This meant writing in my Gratitude Journal daily and really *feeling* the feelings of being grateful for these things, as if I already had them.

I was living in Sydney at the time, and I wanted to get away to make a completely fresh start. I also wanted a boyfriend and a new job that I enjoyed.

I met a guy from Melbourne, and we got along really well right away. It all happened very quickly and in a way I'd never have anticipated. Because he had to go back to Melbourne and I lived in Sydney, we had to rely on telephone calls, texts, and emails for communication. We spoke on the phone every single day, and after only four weeks, he asked me if I'd like to move down to Melbourne to live with him. Even though it had been such a short time, it felt right, so I did it.

Once I got to Melbourne, I began to contact employment agencies, looking for a job. I had already written down what I wanted in a job, and I had used The Secret principles. After I initially took a couple of temporary positions just to earn some money, a fantastic job came up. It met all the criteria that I had set for the ideal job and turned out to be the best job I'd ever had.

I also printed out the check from The Secret website, pinned it on my vision board, and focused on having received the money and feeling good about prosperity. Very soon afterward, my father called me, very excited to let me know he had won quite a bit of money in Powerball! He told me that he wanted me to have some of it and that he'd be sending a check for five thousand dollars!

I was very happy with my boyfriend and with my job. I loved living in Melbourne and I loved our house. The next thing I put on my vision board was children. I so wanted children, and I'd always wanted twin girls. I cut out a picture of newborn twin girls from a magazine and put it on my vision board. I was also buying baby clothes in advance, and I'd buy two of everything (newborn girls' clothes). Again, I used principles from *The Secret* and got into feeling that what I wanted was already a reality.

Less than eight weeks after moving to Melbourne, I discovered I was pregnant. Morning sickness kicked in and was terrible (I'd forgotten to ask about feeling good in the early part of pregnancy!). At twelve weeks, the ultrasound confirmed that we were expecting twins! My boyfriend was surprised, but I knew it was because of The Secret. From then on, I wrote down and believed that I had a very healthy and happy pregnancy (which I did). I got everything I asked for: a healthy pregnancy, a natural birth at thirty-eight weeks, and healthy twin daughters.

I am now studying (through distance education) for a social work degree (another thing I asked for and believed I'd received), I have made many lovely friends, I am happy and financially secure. Lots of amazing little things happen regularly now, and I know it's because I apply The Secret to my whole life.

The Secret changed my life. It will change yours too, if you use it.

~ *Belinda,* Melbourne, Australia

Once Belinda made a definite decision about what she really wanted in life, she put aside her doubts and fears and used all of the practices she'd learned from *The Secret* – including the check from the Universal Bank, a vision board, writing down what she wanted, and keeping a Gratitude Journal – in order to turn her life around and become a person grounded in positivity rather than one who was driven by negative thoughts.

You create through your thoughts and feelings, and no one but you can think your thoughts or feel your feelings.

– The Secret Daily Teachings

FROM THE STREETS TO THE SECRET

For ten years of my life I was a drug-addicted, alcoholic sex worker, spending the last three of those years homeless and not wanting to live anymore. Then I was given *The Secret* to read in an empowerment group I was taking, and I am not kidding when I write that six months after I started using The Secret, my life changed incredibly. I got clean and sober; my daughter and my family came back into my life. I was hired as a day outreach worker at the place where I took the empowerment group and had been given *The Secret*.

Four years later, my life is still incredible. I just opened up my email and found out that I got a job I had been wanting for a long time. My relationship with my daughter, who has been living with me for three years, is wonderful. My life is amazing.

Thank you from the bottom of my heart.

~ *Thea C.,* Victoria, Canada

Everything Is Happening for You

The people in the stories above had difficult early lives. For others, things can appear to be going along well when suddenly a so-called challenge appears. At those times it is important to remind yourself that everything – absolutely everything – is happening *for* you.

> *Good is underneath every single thing that appears to be negative. If we can know that good is all there is, including in a negative situation, then we will see a negative situation turn into all good.*
>
> **– The Secret Daily Teachings**

Maybe, like Kate in the following story, you lost your job and, with it, your confidence in yourself. But whatever the cause, if you start to think of yourself negatively, you'll simply be attracting even more negativity.

A NEW BEGINNING

It began when I was suddenly and unceremoniously made redundant from my job as head of department with a TV company. As the main breadwinner, I knew our house was at risk if I didn't find another well-paid full-time job very soon.

I am a positive person, but the redundancy knocked me for six, and I lost my confidence. I knew it was all about the job being redundant and not the person, but it *felt* like it must have been because of something I had done wrong.

When I'd been job-hunting for three weeks, I saw *The Secret* reviewed in *The Observer*. It felt like something I would enjoy reading, and I made a mental note to buy the book when it was published, but along with several other must-dos, I didn't.

Then, by "chance," I was coming back from yet another interview that clearly wasn't going anywhere when I picked up a copy of *The London Evening Standard* that someone had left on the train. I started reading, and there was an excerpt from *The Secret*. I had not had a good day, and this felt like a nudge from "upstairs," so as soon as I got off the train, I went straight to the local bookshop to buy a copy.

As soon as I got home, I began to read and started the visualization exercises. I told the Universe I was ready to receive. Just as I finished reading the book at 5:30 p.m. (I had not put it down), the phone rang, and it was the deputy managing director of the company I wanted to work for – not a personal assistant, not a recruiter, the deputy managing director – asking me if I would be kind enough to attend an interview with him and the CEO the next day at 9:30 a.m.!

I was quite amazed and excited and dashed out of the house to meet my partner at the bus stop to tell him all about the book and the call. On the way home, a friend we hadn't seen in a while, who worked at the local Italian restaurant, popped her head up from over a bush and invited us to come into the restaurant for a bottle of champagne – for no reason at all.

That night I imagined the drive to the interview, the interview going well, and the job being mine. The drive was fine. The normally heavy traffic was light. The interview was good but very long. The offer letter arrived the next day, and the package was 20 percent better than what I'd had at my old job!

I stayed happily in that job for five years and then moved on. *The Secret* stayed on the shelf until, out of the blue, my partner of nine years left me. I was devastated. In my heart, I didn't feel it was over. I took *The Secret* down from the bookshelf and began to read and reread it. I also downloaded the film and played it on my daily commute, visualizing us happy together.

Visualizing was really hard. It felt wrong that we were apart, but I couldn't say why.

About fifteen months after leaving, my partner came home. It was wonderful, and we took things gently. My work was manic, and he was there for me. Seven months later, at one o'clock in the morning, I found out why my soul knew he had to be home.

Without any warning, I had a heart attack and went into cardiac arrest.

My partner performed CPR until the paramedics arrived and stayed with me while I was in an induced coma for three days. He has been there for my *full* recovery.

I knew, and I visualized him home. I followed my truth. And now? Once again The Secret is working for me. See it, believe it, make it happen.

After my cardiac arrest, I knew things had to change – I am still working as a full-time TV producer and I love it, but I am also training to qualify as a clinical hypnotherapist and cognitive behavioral therapy executive coach and speaker, which I've always wanted to do but never thought I could.

But I saw it, visualized it, and made the time for the foundation course and the professional course (evenings and weekends), as well as the time to study, practice, and qualify.

My partner and I are still together with our two grumpy eleven-year-old rescue cats and our nine-month-old very happy puppy.

It does work: smile and you can't be sad. Be grateful and thankful and generate more good things in your life!

~ *Kate L.*, London, England

Each time Kate visualized what she wanted, the Universe responded by delivering exactly what she asked for, even down to her partner returning home. Because we can never override another person's freedom to choose for themselves, Kate's partner had to want the same thing in order for it to manifest. Kate and her partner were clearly a match!

THE VIEW FROM LIFE'S CROSSROADS

I am overwhelmed with inspiration – inspiration to share my story as it once was and as it is today. The peace of mind I now have from the understanding that I am creator of my story has and will continue to transform my life. I am experiencing a level of gratitude right now that I have never felt before this moment.

I am thirty-one years old, and I am a recovering heroin and cocaine addict.

Three and a half years ago I was, by many people's standards, living an exceptional life. I had found the love of my life and conceived the most inspiring and beautiful person I have ever known, Tayven, my son. I was living in a beautiful home. I owned two great vehicles and a Harley-Davidson. I was living what many would call the American dream.

It was through my lack of gratitude for the amazing things I had in my life that I "lost it all," or, as I now say, "gave it all away." We have all heard the saying many times that "a person doesn't know what he has until it's gone." I now like to say that a person knows what he has; he just is not grateful for it until it's gone.

Looking back, I am amazed that I ever felt any level of success. Yes, I became very good at acquiring material things, but I never took the time to appreciate what was really important – my ability to create them and all the other circumstances I had experienced. I felt no gratitude for the people who supported me in creating these things, or for the opportunities that were literally thrown in front of me to create an astonishing existence.

I am so very grateful for the new perspective on life I have gained as a result of giving up everything I have ever loved and worked for. Only through "starting from scratch," as they say, can I truly see how blessed I have been.

I was released from jail after serving a year in custody. I am now a convicted felon after being found in possession of heroin and cocaine. You see, I not only felt ungrateful for the things and people in my life, I also felt I was entitled to experience them while I was intoxicated.

I spent much of the first six or so months of my incarceration blaming outside people and circumstances for my situation. It wasn't until I read *The Secret* and started adopting its principles of looking inward to change and taking ownership for my life that it truly started to transform. This amazing book found its way into my life at the most opportune time. I was quite literally standing at a crossroads where my life could have taken two dramatically different paths.

After four near-death overdoses, a pulmonary embolism, and a year of my life behind bars, I can truly say thank you, not only to the amazing team who created this book but also to the Universe for bringing into my life exactly what I was asking for. Even though what I was asking for was not pleasant, it was granted. I am so grateful for the opportunity to have survived, and for the chance to start asking for the right things in my life.

I am a perfect example of what an amazing experience using The Secret can be for anyone brave enough to look at their own life – the result of what they have attracted into it. I want nothing more than for all of mankind to experience the level of optimism and gratitude I am feeling today.

~ *Avery H.,* Salt Lake City, Utah, USA

Gratitude: The Life-Changer

For some people, gratitude seems to come naturally. It takes others longer to appreciate the key role that gratitude plays in the law of attraction. In the end, however, no matter the difficulty of the situation in which you may find yourself, practicing gratitude will help you find a way out.

UNDERSTANDING WHAT IT MEANS TO BE GRATEFUL

I can't really explain it. I had wanted to understand what *The Secret* really meant about being grateful for everything you have and for everything you want. I wasn't sure I would be able to do it. For two weeks after I bought them, I read the book and listened to the CD over and over. I've wanted so desperately to try to understand what they were saying and to manifest my own destiny. I didn't realize you couldn't receive anything until you were grateful for what you already had and what you would be receiving.

Things changed all of a sudden when I woke up to my alarm clock one morning and was a little frustrated that I had to get up so early. Immediately, I changed my mood to one of happiness and got out of bed. I was walking in the garden and began to feel the wind against my face and the grass between my toes, and I began to say thank you. I began to thank the Universe for the gift of being me, for my house, my family, being able to enjoy the outdoors. I began to say thank you for everything I could think of, including what I wanted to manifest. I did the same thing for the next two days, and now I finally understand what it's like to be deeply grateful for everything that surrounds you.

I don't have to stop what I'm doing and think about it. I just feel gratitude and happiness and love radiating from me. I used to get angry very easily, but since discovering The Secret, and even more now that I am grateful for everything, very few things upset me, and when they do, I pull myself back and remember that only on a frequency of love, happiness, and gratitude will I receive what I want.

This feeling that beams and radiates inside of me – this feeling that I'm deeply grateful for everything – is one that I wish everyone could learn to feel. The whole world shines. I often see butterflies fluttering in my garden. I am grateful for the birds chirping outside my window, for the wind that blows through my hair, for knowing that what I want is already mine, and for everything. I finally understand that once you are grateful for what surrounds you, you feel peace and love inside, which can only bring you what you want.

~ *Elizabeth M.,* San Diego, California, USA

To create your tomorrow, go over your day tonight when you are in bed, just before you fall asleep, and feel gratitude for the good moments. As you fall asleep, say, "I will sleep deeply and wake up full of energy. Tomorrow is going to be the most beautiful day of my life."

– The Secret Daily Teachings

HOW GRATITUDE SAVED MY LIFE!

I was working in a highly stressful job with unreasonable hours and workload. I was so overwhelmed that I began suffering from severe situational anxiety and panic attacks. My head would spin and my heart would beat rapidly. I would shake, suffer headaches, and panic when I walked into the office. I shut myself away from my friends and family, stopped socializing, exercising, and practicing self-care.

I couldn't cope with not having control over my anxious body and mind; the anxiety had completely taken over all areas of my life. I was desperately unhappy and I couldn't see any escape, so I starting making plans to take my own life.

Yet something stopped me – made me pause and reconsider.

Having watched *The Secret*, and having deep faith in the Universe, I felt called to purchase *The Magic* and began working through the daily gratitude practices.

It was challenging at first, but slowly, it became easier as things in my life began to shift. The changes were small at first, such as a loving text message from a friend, a compliment or social outing that brought me unexpected joy, and then more significant things began to happen.

On day ten, without any previous notice, I was placed on paid stress leave by my employer and given time to rest. By day twenty, I had a clear vision of the type of job I wanted, and amazing career opportunities in my field of expertise kept manifesting. I boldly resigned from my stressful job and never returned to the office.

By day twenty-four, I knew that these practices had saved my life. Having been given time to rest and recuperate, I had the space to think in gratitude and design my order to the Universe for the life I wanted. I trust and believe everything on my list is on its way.

I have gone from being broken and desperate to waking up in a state of euphoric joy each day, and giving thanks for all that I have.

On day twenty-eight of reading and practicing *The Magic*, I was offered my dream job. Not only do the role and the company match all the criteria on my "Universal wish list," but the salary offered is the *exact dollar amount* I wrote on the check from the book. I had goose bumps when I received the formal job offer. I couldn't believe that everything I ordered had been handed to me by the divine Universe!

Thank you, thank you, thank you.

~ *Olivia M.,* Canberra, Australia

Everything You Want Can Be Yours

As each of the following people discovered, whatever you desire, the Universe wants you to have it all.

MIRACLES IN ABUNDANCE!

At the time I came across *The Secret*, my life was a pretty big mess.

I was recovering from an emotional and mental breakdown and various painful addictions, and my relationships were in a state of turmoil. My sister, with whom I was living, was recovering from a paralytic stroke and a broken engagement. She had lost so much weight and become so weak that every day it looked like she wasn't going to make it.

I remember when I first watched *The Secret*, I cried out of happiness. As a child, I always knew that I had the power to shape my life, but I had lost touch with this divine aspect of myself.

From that day on, my life kept changing for the better.

By using and applying The Secret, I moved to a beautiful new home and a new city, away from toxic addictions and energies.

Since then I have applied The Secret to:

- Double my income.

- Quit smoking after being a heavy chain smoker for twenty-three years.

- Heal my troubled emotional issues.

- Free myself of alcohol, substance, and relationship addiction.

- Start a dream business that was in the pipeline for several years.

Most importantly, I am proud of the person I have become: someone who has turned her pain into power. Strong, courageous, and truly joyful, with a new appreciation for love and life!

My sister is also well on her road to recovery, and as for me, I am now applying The Secret to attract the love of my life.

I love this Universe and life and am endlessly grateful for all the miracles The Secret has brought and continues to bring to my life.

~ *R. Lal,* Pune, India

Live your dream on the inside first, completely and totally, and then it will manifest in your life. When you have tuned yourself on the inside so completely, you will magnetize everything you need for your dream to become a reality.

This is the law. All creation in your life begins inside of you.

– The Secret Daily Teachings

MY GREATEST DREAMS CAME TRUE!

I was a single parent for twenty years. I was always worried about money. I never traveled anywhere, nor was I a homeowner. One of my greatest desires and promises to myself was that one day I would travel to the UK. I'd never left North America, and I wanted my first trip abroad to be to London. I also wanted to be a homeowner, and I wanted to feel a sense of financial comfort and ease in my life. But for many years, I saw no way that any of these things would ever happen for me.

Then I came across *The Secret*. I loved it because it inspired me and gave me hope that I could improve my situation once and for all. I also bought *The Power* and then *The Magic*, and I began focusing on what I loved and practicing gratitude every single day.

I really wanted to saturate my body, mind, and spirit with love, gratitude, and the belief that I could improve my life. Something in me knew that repetition was the key. Just keep reading those books, keep practicing gratitude, keep watching those videos, keep strengthening my belief.

It worked. It still brings me to tears sometimes when I think about just how well it worked for me.

Over time, I increased the intensity of my gratitude and visualization exercises. I began doing my exercises twice a day – first thing when I woke up every morning and last thing before I fell asleep every night – for thirty days straight.

The result? Within six months, the following amazing improvements happened in my life:

• My son graduated from university, found the job he wanted, and moved into his own home. What a wonderful reward to see him so healthy, happy, and successful in his own life.

- My annual income from my job increased by $30,000.

- I also earned some extra money through my sideline home business.

- I was approved for a mortgage, bought myself a brand-new condo with many luxuries, including safe and secure underground parking, and moved in.

- I booked myself a trip to London and Paris using a credit card and knowing I could pay it off within six months because of my increase in income.

- I gave my son all my old furniture and was easily able to afford new furniture for my new condo to be financed over three years.

- I bought myself a new Jeep, to be financed over six years.

- Then my mother won $1.15 million in a casino lottery in Prince Albert, Saskatchewan! She generously shared part of her winnings with her children, which allowed me to pay off all my debt, including the trip to London and Paris, the new Jeep, the new furniture, everything! Except for my mortgage, I was completely debt-free; I had savings put away and even more spending money at my disposal.

- Not only did my mother win the casino lottery, but amazingly, two months later, my uncle (who happens to be my godfather) won $1.4 million in a separate casino lottery in Medicine Hat, Alberta!

- On top of all that, I decided to take a long-desired trip to New York City.

- Not only did every wish I had for myself come true, but even better, I got to see my son and my mom enjoy success and joy in their own lives. God, that felt good!

My life continues to be so fulfilling. I continue to earn a great living and travel. I continue to have a wonderful relationship with my son and watch him have success in his own life. It's wonderful.

I'm so grateful to you, Rhonda. You have helped me to change my life for the better. Thank you, thank you, thank you!

~ *Kim S.,* Canada

We can't control every single thing that comes into our lives, because our lives involve other people, and we can't control their actions. But as Charlotte so eloquently put it in the following story, we can always control *how we respond* to what happens in our life.

OVERCOMING MANY LOSSES

Over the past twelve years, there has been a great deal of loss in my life. My mother, all four of my uncles, two aunts, four family friends, and two beloved pets have passed over. My most recent loss was my very special little cat, Renny, who died this spring at the age of fourteen. My only remaining family members are my eighty-seven-year-old father and one sister.

Before *The Secret*, if someone had told me I'd be suffering so much loss in such a relatively short time, I would have been convinced it would completely destroy me. I can't deny that I've felt very grieved, lonely, and heartbroken when these losses occurred, and I have shed many tears. I've also struggled with anxiety and depression in the wake of several of these deaths.

But thanks to *The Secret* and the law of attraction, I have been able to overcome my grief each time and bounce back to life in a much shorter time than I would have believed possible. In fact, as counterintuitive as it may seem given the losses I've just described, I've actually been enjoying life more in recent years than I ever did before! I feel stronger, and life just seems richer and more interesting and exciting.

The Secret was a revelation to me because it taught me that we don't have to be victims of our circumstances or emotions. I used to believe that we can't help what happens to us or even how we react to it. I lived in constant fear, wondering when the next crisis was going to strike and send me into an emotional tailspin. I also used to make my happiness dependent on what others did or didn't do. Learning that I can't control others but that I can control my reactions to what they do was a real "aha!" moment for me. So was the realization that I can control my future by what I attract through my thoughts and emotions, whether good or bad.

I know I can't stop the elderly people and pets in my life from dying, but *The Secret* taught me that I can control how I respond to these events. Whether I go into an emotional collapse, clinging to the past and wishing for the impossible, or calmly let my loved ones go and accept their passing as part of their own spiritual journey while looking to the future for better things, is entirely up to me. What an empowering concept!

Each time I've suffered a loss or other setback, I've rewatched *The Secret* to help me recharge my batteries and regain my strength and enthusiasm for life. It works every time. It doesn't happen overnight, of course, but I know that I'd be in a bad place today if not for The Secret.

~ *Charlotte B.,* Ontario, Canada

Every person who told their story in this book had no motivation other than a great desire to uplift and inspire *you*. Sometimes their story involved suffering; as you've seen, it can often be that the greater the suffering, the greater the impetus to change our life completely. From the ashes comes new life.

It is never too late to change anything or everything; there is no point that is too low to come back from. There is no opportunity that is lost. And the great news is that it's not the world you need to change. Just change the way you think, change the way you feel, and the world as you know it will change before your eyes. It will then be *your* story that uplifts and inspires others; through changing yourself, you will indeed go on to change the world.

WRESTLING WITH THE SECRET

At twenty-two years old I landed my dream job as a professional wrestler. Although the job had me working my way through a minor league of sorts, I hoped to make it to the big time. Wrestling was all I had ever wanted to do since I was twelve years old. I loved the physicality. I loved learning. But this job environment turned out to be something different; it was a whole new world of mental and physical abuse that took pride in breaking people's spirits.

Slowly and without even realizing it, I was becoming more and more negative and was losing hope with each passing day. I lost my confidence because of all the negativity around me and inside of me. I didn't quit, as I don't have that in me, and I would show spurts of turning it around. But then, *bam*! Something would knock me down again.

Just when I didn't think things could get any worse, they of course did: I was transferred to a different city and spent what was without a doubt the most difficult year of my adult life at my new job in a new city. While things improved from a physical standpoint with my wrestling, I was mentally defeated. I had no real goals set for myself and was just letting life control me. I would watch the news and be depressed. I would go to the gym and be depressed. I would sit around and drink with some of the guys on off nights and wake up even more depressed. Negativity was ruling my world. I started having nightmares every single night that I was going to be fired from my once dream job.

One day at training, I was talking with my best friend, Pat. Pat was an unpaid walk-on athlete trying every day just to get to the paid, contracted position I already had. On this day, we were stretching and warming up around the ring, getting ready for practice. "I bet I get fired today," I muttered. Pat looked up: "You're not getting fired. You're the biggest guy in here with the most potential." Still, the negativity pressed on.

Then everyone in the locker room heard a rumor that three people were about to be released from their contracts. I went home in a somber mood after a grueling training day and elected to take a nap to escape my problems. I woke up to a voicemail from my boss. I was fired.

I was so ashamed of myself for losing what had been my dream job that I absolutely hit rock bottom. I moved in with a girl I had met very early on and eventually landed a job at Smokey Bones restaurant. I slaved there for fifty to sixty hours a week, and even though I enjoyed the work, I missed wrestling. It felt a little better when I got Pat hired and

we could at least talk about our wrestling dreams and our
failures.

I began to let alcohol and chewing tobacco take hold of my
life in a very bad way.

Every night after work, I would buy a bottle of vodka and sit
around and drink. At first it seemed harmless because I was
doing it with my girlfriend, but eventually, we broke up, and
I sank even lower. I now had no dream job and no girlfriend.
I went from living in her large beautiful house to living in a
rundown studio apartment with nothing but a TV, a cheap
bed, and a couch she was kind enough to let me borrow. I was
so ashamed that I avoided speaking to my parents, and I didn't
go home for almost two years.

Pat was really concerned to see the way I was living, and
since he was going through a parallel story with a bad
breakup, we agreed to find an affordable apartment near our
job and hopefully one day get back to chasing our wrestling
dream. While I was at work one day, an old friend whom I
hadn't seen in a long time came into the restaurant. He was
devastated to see me in my current situation, and before
he left, he told me he had read a book called *The Secret*
and it had helped him a lot. He gave me some money and

said, "Go buy this book today. It will help you." I figured it wouldn't hurt, so I went out and purchased my copy of *The Secret*. I got home that night and read the entire book in one sitting. It instantly captivated me! It hit me that as a child, I had actually used a lot of the principles in my thinking, but in adulthood, I had lost that positive "I can do anything I want" mind-set. I read the book again, and I went out and purchased *The Secret* DVD and got a vision board to visualize all of my goals.

Pat was working the late shift, and when he came home, I told him about *The Secret*. He was immediately interested. I think he saw something had woken up inside of me. Pat watched the video, read the book, and got a vision board as well. Our whole apartment became a visualization piece for our future; there were motivating images and posters all around.

Within a month, Pat asked me to come with him and wrestle at some events to get back into the game. I agreed, and we were back in the mix of things. It felt fun. It felt positive. Sure, we were still working long hours at a restaurant, but our energy changed.

One day while I was watching *Terminator 2*, a realization hit me. I felt like Arnold! I felt invincible; I felt that I had been through enough to be a Terminator-type character. I gave myself this new identity, and with the knowledge of The Secret, I was ready for round two at my dream job.

Well, long story wrapped up, I impressed my old bosses and ended up getting my dream job back. Before long, I made it to the big time, and now everything I could have ever dreamed of wanting in life has come my way!

There is so much more, but this is the essence of a true story about a twelve-year-old boy named Ryan Reeves who had a dream to become a professional wrestler. He lost that dream, then discovered The Secret and got the dream back, and today he is proud to be known worldwide as WWE Superstar, the Big Guy – Ryback!

As for Pat, he now owns two professional wrestling companies, two training schools, and has done incredible things with his life. Seven years ago we were living in a small, smoky apartment, depressed and defeated. It's amazing what this knowledge can do.

~ *Ryan R.*, Las Vegas, Nevada, USA

Our natural state of being is joy. It takes so much energy to think negative thoughts, to speak negative words, to feel miserable. The easy path is good thoughts, good words, and good deeds. Take the easy path.

– The Secret Daily Teachings

To get everything you want is an inside job! The outside world is the world of effects; it's just the result of thoughts. Think and bask in happy thoughts. Radiate the feelings of happiness and joy, and transmit that into the Universe with all of your might, and you will experience true heaven on earth.

Keys To Changing Your Life

- *You deserve all the good things life has to offer. Whatever you desire, the Universe wants you to have it.*

- *Treat yourself the way you want others to treat you.*

- *If you think of yourself negatively, you'll attract negative circumstances to you.*

- *Life is mirroring back to you what you are feeling inside.*

- *All creation in your life begins inside of you.*

- *Live the life you dream of having on the inside first, and then it will manifest.*

- *Even though it might not appear so at times, everything is happening for you.*

- *No matter what difficult situation you find yourself in, practicing gratitude will help you find a way out.*

- *It's not what happens to you but how you respond to what happens in your life.*

- *It is never too late to change anything or everything — change the way you think, change the way you feel.*

Acknowledgments

It's an honor to express my sincere gratitude to the following people for their support and contributions to this very special book:

To the amazing contributors who shared their Secret Stories with the singular intent that their story would help and inspire other people, I thank you with all my heart. And to the tens of thousands of people who have shared their Secret Stories on our website – thank you!

The creation of this book was a team effort, and because of that it was an absolute joy to work on from beginning to end. I would like to thank the Secret Team members for their dedication and invaluable contributions. We're a relatively small team, but a fantastically talented group of people. On the editorial side, producer Paul Harrington and editor Skye

Byrne painstakingly worked side by side with me on the creation of this book. They are as much a part of its pages as I am. To super-duper organizer Glenda Bell, CFO, and downright good person Don Zyck, social media champ Josh Gold, Secret Stories website editor and dear friend Marcy Koltun-Crilley, thank you all.

For the cover of the book and the interior styling, my thanks to the very talented artist and creative director for *The Secret,* Nic George. My thanks also to the art director for Atria Books, Albert Tang, who worked in conjunction with Nic on the book cover.

To our wonderful publishing partner, Simon & Schuster, and in particular, the team at Atria Books. My thanks to the president of Atria Books, fellow Australian and special human being Judith Curr, along with the best group of people you could hope to work with under the Atria production umbrella: Lisa Keim, Darlene DeLillo, Rakesh Satyal, Loan Le, Kimberly Goldstein, Paige Lytle, Jim Thiel, Isolde Sauer, E. Beth Thomas, Carly Sommerstein, Dana Sloan, and writer Judith Kern. Thank you so very much to all of you!

To Carolyn Reidy, CEO of Simon & Schuster – thank you!

To our legal team, Bonnie Eskenazi, Julia Haye, and Jesse Savoir of Greenburg Glusker. And at Atria Books, Elisa M. Rivlin.

I have received life-changing realizations through many, many spiritual teachers and traditions over the last ten years. In particular, I want to thank my constant mentor and friend, Angel Martin Velayos of the Rose Cross Order, and the teachers who have impacted my spiritual understanding during the creation of this book; Sailor Bob Adamson (love ya, Bob), Robert Adams, and David Bingham.

To my precious family: my very special daughters, Hayley and Skye Byrne; beautiful sisters, Pauline Vernon, Glenda Bell, and Jan Child; Peter Byrne and Oku Den, Kevin "Kid" McKemy, Paul Cronin, and my gorgeous grandchildren, Savannah and Henley. I am extremely blessed to have each one of them.

To some of my dearest and longtime friends who remain so despite my single-minded desire to discuss spiritual truths at every possible moment: Elaine Bate, Mark Weaver, and Fred Nalder, Forrest Kolb, Andrea Keir, and Kathy Kaplan. And to a special group of people I have the pleasure to connect with through business who help make life even more wonderful: Robert Cort, the amazing Kevin Murphy and Negin Zand, Dani Piola, my personal assistant Pamela Vandervort, Eileen Randall, and Eligia Trujillo.

Finally, you would not be holding this book in your hands if it were not for my daughter Skye. She not only edited and worked on this book, she initiated the Secret Stories as a publishing project, and enthusiastically urged this project on at every turn until its final creation. The result is that it's one of the best books we've ever published – because it's from people just like you.

Contributors by Country

Jessica T., Vancouver, British Columbia, Canada
BEAUTIFUL HEALING, page 125

Dallas C., Winnipeg, Manitoba, Canada
TWO WEEKS TO A NEW LIFE, page 192

Kim S., Canada
MY GREATEST DREAMS CAME TRUE!, page 235

Mrs. Abundant, Ottawa, Ontario, Canada
WRITE YOUR OWN CHECK, page 73

Roland C., Nanaimo, Canada
WHEN THERE'S A WILL, THERE'S A WAY!, page 179

Thea C., Victoria, Canada
FROM THE STREETS TO THE SECRET, page 219

Europe

Andrea, Ireland
THE POWER OF VISION, page 142

Evangelia K., Athens, Greece
TRUE LOVE OUT OF THE BLUE!, page 104

Middle East

United Kingdom

Marta, Mississippi
POPEYE, page 13

Ryan R., Las Vegas, Nevada
WRESTLING WITH THE SECRET, page 242

Carol S., Syracuse, New York
WAKE-UP CALL, page 132

Hannah, New York, New York
THE BEST YEAR OF MY LIFE, page 46

Heather M., Buffalo, New York
NEW HOUSE, NEW BABY, page 53

Kate, Long Island, New York
WHAT GETS YOU TO BELIEVE?, page 169

Maria, New York
AT TWENTY-FIVE YEARS OLD, I GOT MY BOOK
PUBLISHED!!!, page 174

Franci K., Doylestown, Pennsylvania
KYLE'S HEART, page 153

Follow The Secret

Instagram: @thesecret365

Facebook: facebook.com/thesecret/

Twitter: @thesecret